# BUILDING YOUR MARRIAGE

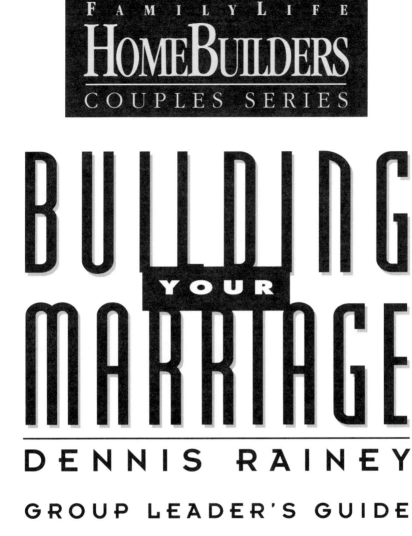

# FAMILY LIFE
# HOMEBUILDERS
## COUPLES SERIES

# BUILDING
## YOUR
# MARRIAGE

## DENNIS RAINEY

### GROUP LEADER'S GUIDE

"UNLESS THE LORD BUILDS THE HOUSE
THEY LABOR IN VAIN WHO BUILD IT."
Psalm 127:1

Gospel Light

# How to
# Let the Lord
# Build Your House
## *and not labor in vain*

**FamilyLife** is a part of Campus Crusade for Christ International, an evangelical Christian organization founded in 1951 by Bill Bright. FamilyLife was started in 1976 to help fulfill the Great Commission by strengthening marriages and families and then equipping them to go to the world with the gospel of Jesus Christ. Our FamilyLife Marriage Conference is held in most cities throughout the United States and is one of the fastest-growing marriage conferences in America today. Information on all resources offered by FamilyLife may be obtained by either writing or calling us at the address and telephone number listed below.

■

**The HomeBuilders Couples Series:** A small-group Bible study dedicated to making your family all that God intended.

**Building Your Marriage—Leader's Guide**
ISBN 0-8307-1613-0

Dennis Rainey, Director
**FamilyLife**
P.O. Box 23840
Little Rock, AR 72221-3840
(501) 223-8663

**A Ministry of Campus Crusade for Christ International**
Bill Bright, Founder and President

Published by Gospel Light, Ventura, California 93006

**To Jerry and Sheryl Wunder,**
because your friendship, servanthood and lives
have made **The HomeBuilders Couples Series** a reality.

# CONTENTS

# ACKNOWLEDGMENTS

The following Bible study is a result of the vision and labor of a team of individuals committed to strengthening marriages around the world. While I owe many thanks to the entire FamilyLife staff, a few "heroes" deserve special recognition.

First, my friend and colleague Jerry Wunder has been, in many ways, the heart behind this entire project. His unwavering belief in this study has endured months of writing, testing and final reworking.

Bob Horner played an instrumental role throughout this process through his vital conceptual and content advice. Robert Lewis, Bill McKenzie and Lee Burrell also made significant contributions toward the content of the Bible study. For help during its earliest stages, I must also thank Mark Dawson and Mike Rutter.

As the study neared completion, a few of our staff emerged as true "champions of the cause." First, there is Julie Denker, whose writer's touch added clarity and definition to my periodic ramblings! And then there are Jeff Lord, who served faithfully as my researcher, and Fred Hitchcock, with his indispensable editing abilities. And finally, there is Donna Guirard and her finishing touches on the "look" and design of the series.

Julie and Jeff also spent many hours at the word processor entering seemingly endless revisions. Tim Allen and Brenda Harris also were a help in the final stages with word processing. As always, Jeff Tikson pitched in, especially when I became ill, and pushed the study through to the end.

Don and Sally Meredith have also influenced our ministry and our lives in so many ways and, as a result, leave a legacy through this study.

There were many groups—around the country—who participated in pilot home studies. Thanks for your feedback. It was invaluable.

And last, I need to extend a heartfelt word of appreciation to Wes Haystead. Thank you, Wes, for coming alongside our team and helping to make this dream a reality.

# INTRODUCTION

## ABOUT THE HOMEBUILDERS COUPLES SERIES

### What is the purpose of the HomeBuilders Series?

Do you remember the first time you fell in love? That junior high—or elementary school—"crush" stirred your affections with little or no effort on your part. We use the term "falling in love" to describe the phenomenon of suddenly discovering our emotions have been captured by someone delightful.

Unfortunately, our society tends to make us think that all loving relationships should be equally as effortless. Thus, millions of couples, Christians included, approach their marriage certain that the emotions they feel will carry them through any difficulties. And millions of couples quickly learn that a good marriage does not automatically happen.

Otherwise intelligent people, who would not think of buying a car, investing money, or even going to the grocery store without some initial planning, enter into marriage with no plan of how to make their marriage succeed.

But God has already provided the plan, a set of blueprints for a truly godly marriage. His plan is designed to enable two people to grow together in a mutually satisfying relationship, and then to look beyond their own marriage to others. Ignoring this plan leads to isolation and separation between husband and wife—the pattern so evident in the majority of homes today. Even when great energy is expended, failure to follow God's blueprints results in wasted effort, bitter disappointment—and, in far too many cases, divorce.

In response to this need in marriages today, FamilyLife of Campus Crusade for Christ has created a series of small-group Bible studies for couples called The HomeBuilders Couples Series. The series is designed for small-group studies and is easily adaptable to larger groups such as adult Sunday School classes. It is planned to answer one question for couples:

How do you build a distinctively Christian marriage?

It is our hope that in answering this question with the biblical blueprints for building a home, we will see the development of growing, thriving marriages filled with the love of Jesus Christ.

FamilyLife of Campus Crusade for Christ is committed to strengthening your family. We hope The HomeBuilders Couples Series will assist you and your church as it equips couples in building godly homes.

## What is this study intended to accomplish?

Couples who participate in these sessions will find that the experience:

- Stimulates them to examine what Scripture says about how to construct a solid, satisfying marriage.
- Allows them to interact with each other on a regular basis about significant issues in their marriages.
- Encourages them to interact with other couples, establishing mutual accountability for growth efforts.
- Motivates them to take specific actions which have been valuable to couples desiring to build stronger homes.
- Creates accountability to others for growth in their marriages.

## Why is accountability so important?

Accountability is a scriptural principle that tells us to "be subject to one another in the fear of Christ" (Ephesians 5:21). This means I choose to submit my life to the scrutiny of another person in order to gain spiritual strength, growth and balance.

Accountability means asking another person for advice. It means giving him the freedom to make honest observations and evaluations about you. It means you're teachable and approachable. True accountability involves letting another person into the interior of your life.

When a person joins a small group, he is opening himself up for at least a small measure of accountability. Our experience has shown that many group members will make commitments to apply aspects of the studies to their lives, but will never follow through on those commitments. As a small-group leader, establishing an environment of friendly accountability can help your group members get the most out of this study.

Look for some hints on establishing accountability in the "Tips for Leading Your Group" section.

## What impact has The HomeBuilders Couples Series had in marriages?

Since we published the first HomeBuilders study in 1987, we've continually heard stories about couples whose marriages were revitalized and, in some cases, even saved. Here are some examples:

> "We started our HomeBuilders group as a follow-up to the Video FamilyLife Conference presented at our church. We have developed a good openness among the group members. It has brought problem areas to the surface and given us a greater sense of awareness of our responsibility toward our mate. One couple travels as far as an hour to attend!"
>
> Pastor, Washington

> "We're using *Building Your Marriage* and *Mastering Your Money in Marriage* in our Sunday school classes, both for newlyweds and as a marriage renewal class. I have seen couples open communication lines for the first time in a long time as a result of their involvement."
>
> Bill Willits
> Minister to Married Adults
> First Baptist Church
> Atlanta, Ga.

> "We've led three studies now, and in each one of those we have seen ourselves grow. You really do co-learn."
>
> Doug Grimm
> Playa Del Rey, Calif.

> "I've built my family ministry around the FamilyLife Conference and the HomeBuilders. It makes biblically-mind-

ed, servant-minded people who are useful for advancing the kingdom and leadership of the kingdom."

Jeff Rhodes, pastor
First Presbyterian Church
Winterhaven, Fla.

"Nine weeks of the HomeBuilders class turned everything around in our relationship. It was a real miracle. The walls came down and the masks came off. We were able to discuss matters we had swept under the carpet years ago that our enemy was consistently using to destroy the love God had designed for us since the beginning of time....

"The HomeBuilders class really works. Here is why: HomeBuilders not only shows you why, and tells you how, it teaches a way to alter your life-style so these great truths become a part of everyday living.

"We have truly overcome isolation and are building toward oneness in our marriage. We have learned how to yield to God and the leading of His Holy Spirit instead of our own selfish desires...the romance is back and the intimacy is growing every day. HomeBuilders has really given us the 'wisdom' we were looking for in our marriage.

"It is absolutely the best thing that has ever happened to us since becoming Christians 18 years ago. It changed our lives at a time I was just ready to accept apathy for parts of my marriage, figuring there was no way to ever change."

Alan and Lanette Hauge
Playa Del Rey, Calif.

## How does this study fit into a strategy for building Christian marriages?

While this study has great value in itself, it is only the first step in a long-term process of growth. If people complete these sessions and then gradually return to their previous patterns of living, little or no good will result. Continued effort is required for people to initiate and maintain new directions in their marriages.

It is our belief, also, that no couple can truly build a Christian home and marriage without a strong commitment and involvement in a local church. The church provides the daily spiritual direction and equipping necessary for a truly godly marriage.

FamilyLife is committed to changing the destiny of the family and providing quality resources to churches and individuals to build distinctively Christian marriages. In addition to The Home-Builders Couples Series, we offer:

- "FamilyLife Today," our daily radio show with Dennis Rainey. This half-hour broadcast offers biblical, practical tips for building your family with a foundation in Christ.
- The FamilyLife Marriage Conference, a weekend getaway for couples to learn how to experience oneness in their marriages.
- The FamilyLife Parenting Conference, in which parents learn practical ways to raise their children to know and love the Lord.
- The Urban Family Conference, a shorter version of the FamilyLife Marriage Conference that is geared to the needs of African-American families.
- Numerous materials to help you grow as a family and reach out to others.

## Can this study be used in other settings besides small groups?

Yes! With capable leadership, this study may be used effectively in other settings. For example:

- A counselor could use it with a couple.
- Two couples who know each other well could work through it together.
- You could go through the study with your mate. (We encourage you, however, to make your ultimate goal that of taking others through this study, or participating in a small group. Accountability is essential for godly marriages.)
- A Sunday School leader can adapt it to a larger group setting. For some suggestions on how this can be done, refer to the section titled, "Using This Study in a Sunday School Setting."

## Does each session follow a format?

Yes. The following outline gives a quick look at how the sessions are structured:

**FOCUS:** a statement of the overall focus of the session you will be studying.

**WARM UP:** a time to help people get to know each other, review the past session and begin the new study.

**BLUEPRINTS:** the biblical content of the session.

**CONSTRUCTION:** the application of the session—a small project done privately as a couple during the session.

**HOMEBUILDERS PRINCIPLES:** summary points made throughout the study.

**MAKE A DATE:** a time for couples to decide when they will complete their **HomeBuilders Project**.

**HOMEBUILDERS PROJECT:** a 60-90 minute project to be completed at home before the next session.

**RECOMMENDED READING:** suggestions for use of several books to get maximum value from the study.

Although this format may vary slightly from session to session, you should familiarize yourself with it so that you are aware of the purpose of each segment of the study. Explaining the segments to your group will also aid them in understanding the session's content.

## How is the Bible used in this study?

As you proceed through this study, you will notice that the Bible is regarded as the final authority on the issues of life and marriage. Although written centuries ago, this Book still speaks clearly and powerfully about the conflicts and struggles men and women face. The Bible is God's Word and contains His blueprints for building a godly home and for dealing with the practical issues of living.

While Scripture has only one primary interpretation, there may be several appropriate applications. Some of the passages used in this series were not originally written with marriage in mind, but they can be applied practically to the husband-wife relationship.

Encourage each group member to have a Bible with him for each session. *The New American Standard Bible*, the *New International Version®* and the *New King James Version* are three excellent English versions which make the Bible easy to understand.

## What are the ground rules for these sessions?

These sessions are designed to be enjoyable and informative—and nonthreatening. Three simple ground rules will help ensure that everyone feels comfortable and gets the most out of the study:

1. Share nothing about your marriage which will embarrass your mate.
2. You may "pass" on any question you do not want to answer.
3. Complete the **HomeBuilders Projects** (questions for each couple to discuss and act on) between each session. Share one result at the next group meeting.

## What is the purpose of this leader's guide?

This book and the suggestions we make are designed to cause your creative juices to flow, not cramp your style. You will undoubtedly come up with some creative ways to instruct and teach this material. That's fine. Don't let these recommendations force you into a box.

If, however, you find it difficult to be creative as a facilitator, this guide will relieve your fears. In it you will find ideas, questions and tips that will help you keep the study moving.

The entire text of the study guide (including **Construction** and **HomeBuilders Projects**) is reprinted here, along with the tips for the leader and answers to the study guide questions. All answers, tips and notes appear in italics to distinguish them from the study guide material. As a couple, use this guide to prepare for the session, regardless of the type of leader you are. One good question on a hot topic can spawn great discussion and interaction. Remember, this study is for these couples' marriages and their application.

# TIPS FOR LEADING YOUR GROUP

## What does it take to lead this study?

**First**, you and your mate need to commit to each other and to God that this study will be a major priority for both of you.

**Second**, you will need to work together to enlist other couples to participate in the group.

**Third**, one of you will need to give time (at least one or two hours) each week to prepare for the session while the other takes the initiative to stay in touch with group members and to handle all the details of hospitality.

And **fourth**, we recommended that you pray regularly for each couple in your group.

**NOTE:** Session Five in this study involves separating the husbands and wives into two separate groups. You will need to arrange for someone—your mate or another person—to lead the other group.

## What is the leader's job?

Your role is that of "facilitator"—a directive guide who encourages people to think, to discover what Scripture says and to interact with others in the group. You are not a teacher or lecturer—your job is to help the group members glean biblical truth and apply it to their lives.

At the same time, however, you don't want to let group members ramble aimlessly or pool their ignorance. You'll need to familiarize yourself with the material so that you know where the discussion is headed and so that you can provide answers when needed. The directions in this leader's guide will help you keep each session moving.

## What is the best setting for this group to meet?

Your living room is probably the best place to use for a small group. Inviting couples to your home is usually easier and friendlier than trying to get them to come to a room at church. You need a room where everyone can sit comfortably and see and hear each other.

Avoid letting couples or individuals sit outside the group;

they will not feel included. The seating arrangement is very important to discussion and involvement. If your home will not work, see if another couple in the group is willing to host the sessions.

## What about refreshments?

If you want a comfortable, relaxed setting that encourages people to get to know one another, something to sip and swallow is almost essential. But food should not become the focus of the session. Depending on the time of your meeting, you may find it works well to serve a beverage and light "munchies" as people arrive, then offer a dessert at the close of the study to encourage people to continue talking with each other for a while.

## What time schedule should we plan to follow?

A two-hour block is best. The time for the actual study is 60-90 minutes. The longer time period allows you to move at a more relaxed pace through each part of the session.

Once the people in your group get to know each other and interaction gets underway, you may find it difficult to complete a session in the time allotted. It is not necessary that every question be covered and many are intended to stimulate thought, not to result in exhaustive discussion and resolution of the issue. Be sensitive to your use of time and be careful not to make comments about time pressure which will make the group feel rushed. For example:

■ When you need to move the discussion to the next item, say something like, "We could probably talk about that question the rest of the evening, but we need to consider several other important questions that bear on this issue."

■ When it's necessary to reduce or eliminate the time spent on a later question, simply say, "You can see that there are several more questions we could have moved on to discuss, but I felt we were making real progress, so I chose to spend some extra time on the earlier points."

You will find, as you prepare and review for each session, that some questions or sections are more relevant to your group than other portions of the study. Pace your study in such a way that those questions which must be addressed are not rushed.

*You are the leader* of your group and know the needs of the individual couples best. But keep in mind that the Holy Spirit will have an agenda for couples which you will never know about.

"The mind of man plans his way, but the Lord directs his steps" (Proverbs 16:9). Do your best to prepare and pray over the session and then leave the results to God.

Be sure to protect the application (**Construction**) time at the end of the session. Be aware of the common tendency to avoid taking action by getting embroiled in a discussion. Even if some issues are not fully resolved, encourage people to place the topic on hold and move on to planning specific actions to take. Personal application is at the heart of this study.

Plan up to an additional 30 minutes for fellowship, 5 or 10 minutes of which may precede the study and the remainder afterwards. When you invite people, tell them to plan on the total time. This avoids having people rush off and not get acquainted. During the school year 7:30-9:30 P.M. allows people to get home from work and get baby-sitters if needed.

Also, when you invite people to attend, let them know that the study will go for seven sessions. People like to know for how long they are committing themselves.

**NOTE:** Session Five in this study is different from the others because it requires 30 more minutes for the study, and the husbands and wives will meet in separate groups. Alert people in advance of this longer session so they can make appropriate arrangements for child care, if needed. Or, you may want to divide Session Five into two separate sessions and extend your series to eight sessions.

## How many couples should be in a study group?

Four to seven couples, including you and your mate, is the optimum group size. Fewer than four may put too much pressure on some individuals, stifling their freedom to grow. More than seven will reduce the quality of relationships which can grow among all the couples involved, although there is still ample opportunity for couples to interact with each other and with other couples in the group.

## Whom should we invite to participate?

The concepts in this study will benefit any couple, whether they are newlyweds, engaged, married many years or even just looking ahead to the possibilities of marriage. Leading the group will be easier if your group is made up of couples at similar stages in their relationships. The more they have in common, the easier it will be for them to identify with one another and open up in sharing.

On the other hand, it can also be helpful for a couple to gain a fresh viewpoint on marriage by interacting with a couple having significantly different experiences. In other words, if a couple is interested in building and maintaining a strong marriage, they belong in this study.

## What if one partner doesn't want to participate?

Expect some people, especially some husbands, to attend the first session wishing they were someplace else. Some will be there just because their mate or another couple nagged them to come. Some may be suspicious of a "Bible" study. Others may be fearful of revealing any weaknesses in their marriage. And some may feel either that their marriage is beyond help or that they do not need any help.

You can dispel a great deal of anxiety and resistance at the first session. Simply begin by mentioning that you know there are probably some who came reluctantly. Share a few reasons people may feel that way, and affirm that regardless of why anyone has come, you are pleased each person is there.

Briefly comment on how the concepts in this study have helped you and your marriage and express your confidence that each person will enjoy the study and benefit from it. Also, assure the group that at no time will anyone be forced to share publicly. What each person shares is his or her choice—no one will be embarrassed.

## Can a non-Christian participate in this study?

The study is definitely targeted at Christians, but many non-Christian couples have participated in it. You may find a non-Christian couple or individual who wants to build a strong marriage and is willing to participate. Welcome the non-Christian into your group and seek to get to know the person during the early weeks of the study.

Sometime during the study, schedule a time to meet with this person or couple privately to explain the principles on which this study is built. Share Christ and offer an opportunity to receive Him as Savior and Lord. We recommend "The Four Spiritual Laws" to help you explain how a person can know God. This information is included as an appendix to the study guide and the leader's guide.

## Do you have any suggestions for guiding the discussion?

Keep the focus on what Scripture says, not on you or your ideas—or those of the group members, either. When someone disagrees with Scripture, affirm him or her for wrestling with the issue and point out that some biblical statements are hard to understand or to accept. Encourage the person to keep an open mind on the issue at least through the remainder of the study.

Avoid labeling an answer as "wrong"; doing so can kill the atmosphere for discussion. Encourage a person who gives a wrong or incomplete answer to look again at the question or the Scripture being explored. Offer a comment such as, "That's really close" or, "There's something else we need to see there." Or ask others in the group to respond.

## How can I get all the people in my group to participate in the discussion?

- A good way to encourage a nonparticipator to respond is to ask him or her to share an opinion or a personal experience rather than posing a question that can be answered "yes" or "no" or that requires a specific correct answer.
- The overly talkative person can be kept in control by the use of devices that call for responses in a specific manner (and which also help group members get to know little things about each other):

  "I'd like this question to be answered first by the husband of the couple with the next anniversary."

"...the wife of the couple who had the shortest engagement."

"...any husband who knows his mother-in-law's maiden name."

"...anyone who complained about doing the last session's project."

■ Other devices for guiding responses from the group include:

Go around the group in sequence with each person commenting about a particular question without repeating what anyone else has said.

Ask couples to talk with each other about a question, then have whichever partner has said the least so far in this session report on his or her answer.

Limit answers to one or two sentences—or to 30 seconds each.

## How can I establish an environment of accountability?

From the outset, emphasize the importance of completing the **HomeBuilders Project** after each session. These projects give couples the opportunity to discuss what they've learned and apply it to their lives. The couples who complete these projects will get two or three times as much out of this study as will those who do not.

The most important thing you can do is state at the end of the first session that *at your next meeting you will ask each couple to share something they learned from the HomeBuilders Project. Then, at the next session, follow through on your promise.* If they know you are going to hold them accountable, they'll be more motivated to complete the projects. And they'll be glad they did!

Remember, though, to make this an environment of *friendly* accountability. You should emphasize how beneficial the projects are, and how much persons will grow in their marriage relationship if they complete them. State that you are not here to condemn, but to help. And when you begin the following session by asking each couple what they learned from the project, do it with an attitude of encouragement and forgiveness. Don't seek to embarrass anyone.

One way to establish friendly accountability and to help couples know each other better is to pair up the couples in your group and assign them to be prayer partners or accountability partners. Have them call each other at some point in between group meetings to exchange prayer requests and to see if they've completed their projects.

Another possibility to consider is making a special effort to hold the *men* accountable to be the initiator in completing the projects. You'd need to commit yourself to calling the men in between sessions.

## What should I expect group members to do at the end of these sessions?

As you prepare this study, prayerfully consider each couple in your group and the most appropriate next step to recommend they take when the study is completed:

1. Encourage them to commit to participate in another Home-Builders study, such as *Building Your Mate's Self-Esteem.* (Dennis and Barbara Rainey have coauthored a best-selling book with this same title, *Building Your Mate's Self-Esteem.*) Decide whether you or someone else will lead the study and when you would schedule it. Since some people may not continue to the next study, it may be wise to schedule the other study after several more groups have completed this one. However, if you wait too long, you and your group members may lose the momentum built through this study.

2. Some couples in your group may be candidates to lead their own group in studying *Building Your Marriage.* Raise this possibility, even though their first reaction may be "We don't know enough to be leaders!" Assure them that sharing what they have learned with others is the best way to continue learning. And obviously, if you can lead this study, *they* certainly can as well. Remember, the more cou-

ples who go through this book, the more couples you will have ready for another one.

Expect many to continue on through The HomeBuilders Couples Series. Relationships established during this study will cause most group members to want to continue.

## USING THIS STUDY IN A SUNDAY SCHOOL SETTING

Although this study is currently written for a small-group, home Bible study, with a few minutes of extra planning you can adapt it for a Sunday School class. Here are a few steps to take:

**STEP ONE: Commit yourself to the small-group format.** Many Sunday School classes are geared around a *teacher* format rather than a *small-group* format. In other words, class members learn biblical content from a speaker, and have little interaction with each other. The success of this HomeBuilders study, however, depends upon the small-group dynamic, with class members learning the content by discussing Scriptures themselves and by sharing personal experiences. As leader of the class, you'll need to be committed to making this small-group setting work.

**STEP TWO: Explain to your class how this study is different from others.** Tell them about the small-group format, and about the purpose of the series. Challenge them to commit themselves to coming each week. And explain the need to set aside an hour each week to complete the **HomeBuilders Projects**.

Another difference with a HomeBuilders study is the **Construction** project, in which couples meet individually for a few minutes during the study. While the classroom may not provide visual privacy as couples talk, the sound of numerous couples talking at once make it unlikely anyone will overhear someone's private conversation. In some cases the results of their work are to be shared. In a class situation, this sharing should be done in small groups, or ask for volunteers to share with the full class.

**STEP THREE: Decide how you want to cover all the material in the time you have for Sunday School.** The problem here is simple: These studies are written to last for 60-90 minutes. Most Sunday School classes are an hour long and that time normally includes announcements, singing and prayer. Here are three options to consider:

1. *Eliminate—for just these few weeks—the normal singing and announcements.* If you follow the shorter time guideline for each segment of the sessions, all the content and projects can fit in a 60-minute session.

   People who are used to slipping in late may need an extra nudge to get them there on time. The informal fellowship dimension which is vital to helping people feel at home in the group can be done to a degree before and after the session. The leader will need to be very sensitive to using that time wisely, since people will have other commitments that keep them from lingering.

2. *Look for ways to condense the actual study to about 45 minutes.* One way to accomplish this, of course, is to cut a few questions. Look through each lesson and determine what is most important to cover, and mark the questions that you think could be eliminated. Perhaps you can choose just one question from a **Warm Up** to use, for example.

   If you have more than one small group in your class, another option is to divide questions (or verses) among different groups for discussion, and then have them report briefly on their answers to the whole class.

3. *Divide each session in half and use two weeks of Sunday School for each one.* Go through each session ahead of time and determine a natural stopping place—at the end of one section of **Blueprints,** for example. Then pick up the session at that point next week.

   One thing to consider if you use this option is that you may need to come up with a new **Warm Up** question to use at the beginning of the second week for each session.

**SPECIAL NOTE ABOUT SESSION FIVE IN THIS STUDY:** This session, on roles and responsibilities for husbands and wives, is longer than the others. If you do not want to split this session in half and cover it in successive weeks, we think it will be well worth it to arrange with your class and with church leaders for this one session to extend through the morning church service time. Encourage people to treat this session as something of a "retreat" for these couples.

**STEP FOUR: Determine how you're going to *divide* the class**. If you have less than nine couples, you could have just one group. But if your class is larger, we suggest dividing it. You could either assign each couple to one group that it will meet with during the entire study, or you could divide the class into different groups each week.

**STEP FIVE: Decide how you're going to *direct* the class**. Do you want to appoint a leader for each group or do you prefer guiding the discussion from up front? If you do want to guide the discussion, you could switch back and forth between having the individuals answer questions to the whole class and answering them just within the small groups.

**STEP SIX: Arrange your physical setting.** Use a room where interaction in small groups and couples can easily occur. Leave adequate open space where people can mingle casually before and after the session. Set up chairs around tables or just in circles of six to eight. For variety in some sessions, you may want to set the chairs in a large semicircle (with more than one row if necessary). Avoid straight rows that leave people seeing only the backs of heads.

Plan to occasionally use a chalkboard, overhead projector or flip chart to emphasize key points, to focus attention on key questions or Scriptures and/or to place instructions for assignments to be done by individuals, couples or small groups. Be cautious about overuse of these tools, as they can set a "classroom" tone which may inhibit some people from full participation.

**SPECIAL NOTE ABOUT SESSION FIVE IN THIS STUDY:** In this session you'll divide the husbands and wives into separate groups. If a second room is not available in the church building during the Sunday School hour, we suggest you arrange for either the husbands or wives group to meet in a nearby home or restaurant.

**STEP SEVEN: Decide how you will set up an atmosphere of accountability.** While the **HomeBuilders Projects** are done by couples at home, it is vital that a larger group size does not allow people to escape accountability for completing the assignments. One option is to pair each couple with another couple with whom they will agree to be accountable. Another plan is to divide the class into two or more teams. Each week require couples to turn in an affidavit that they completed their project. Tabulate the results. The team with the lowest completion rate must provide some agreed upon benefit (preferably edible) for the winning team at the end of the series.

# ABOUT THIS
# LEADER'S GUIDE

The entire text of the study guide is included in this book. At the beginning of each session, you'll find some general comments and suggestions. Then, beginning with the **Warm Up**, the text from the study guide is printed in normal type, while comments, answers to questions and tips are printed in italics.

Be sure to read all the leader's guide comments for each session before you lead it.

# HOMEBUILDERS
# PRINCIPLES

**HOMEBUILDERS PRINCIPLE #1:**

It is only as you yield and submit your life to God, obey His Word and deny yourself that you can experience intimacy and build a godly marriage.

**HOMEBUILDERS PRINCIPLE #2:**

Oneness in marriage involves complete unity with each other.

**HOMEBUILDERS PRINCIPLE #3:**

In order to achieve oneness, a couple must share a strong commitment to God's purpose for marriage.

### HOMEBUILDERS PRINCIPLE #4:

When we yield to God
and build together from His
blueprints, we begin the process
of experiencing oneness.

### HOMEBUILDERS PRINCIPLE #5:

The basis for my acceptance
of my mate is faith in God's
character and trustworthiness.

### HOMEBUILDERS PRINCIPLE #6:

A godly marriage is not
created by finding a perfect,
flawless person, but is created
by allowing God's perfect love
and acceptance to flow through
one imperfect person—you—
toward another imperfect
person—your mate.

### HOMEBUILDERS PRINCIPLE #7:

A godly marriage is established
and experienced as we leave,
cleave and become one flesh.

HOMEBUILDERS PRINCIPLE #8:

## Only spiritual Christians can have a hope of building godly homes.

HOMEBUILDERS PRINCIPLE #9:

## The home built by God requires both the husband and wife to yield to the Holy Spirit in every area of their lives.

HOMEBUILDERS PRINCIPLE #10:

## The heritage you were handed is not as important as the legacy you will leave.

HOMEBUILDERS PRINCIPLE #11:

## The legacy you leave is determined by the life you live.

HOMEBUILDERS PRINCIPLE #12:

## Your marriage should leave a legacy of love that will influence future generations.

# MEN ONLY

### HOMEBUILDERS PRINCIPLE FOR MEN #1:

A husband who is becoming a servant-leader is one who is in the process of denying himself daily for his wife.

### HOMEBUILDERS PRINCIPLE FOR MEN #2:

The husband who is becoming an unselfish lover of his wife is one who is putting his wife's needs above his own.

### HOMEBUILDERS PRINCIPLE FOR MEN #3:

The husband who is becoming a caring head of his house is one who encourages his wife to grow and become all that God intended her to be.

# WOMEN ONLY

## HOMEBUILDERS PRINCIPLE FOR WOMEN #1:

**Becoming a successful wife requires that a woman make her husband her number two priority after her relationship with God.**

## HOMEBUILDERS PRINCIPLE FOR WOMEN #2:

**The wife who is becoming an unselfish lover of her husband is one who is putting her husband's needs above her own.**

## HOMEBUILDERS PRINCIPLE FOR WOMEN #3:

**In order for a husband to successfully lead, he must have a wife who willingly submits to his leadership.**

## HOMEBUILDERS PRINCIPLE FOR WOMEN #4:
### A successful wife is one who respects her husband.

# THE HOMEBUILDERS
# COUPLES SERIES

"Unless the Lord builds the house,
they labor in vain who build it."
Psalm 127:1

# OVERCOMING ISOLATION

## OBJECTIVES

You will help your group members adopt God's blueprints for marriage as you guide them to:

- Create some anticipation for your study together;
- Share enjoyable experiences from their marriages;
- Identify selfishness as the cause of isolation in marriage;
- Affirm their awareness that God has a plan for overcoming isolation and selfishness in marriage; and
- Choose a specific step to take to work on defeating selfishness.

## OVERALL COMMENTS

1. This session sets the tone for the series. Take time to become familiar with every item in the session as well as the tips on leading the group found in the introduction to this leader's guide.
2. Be sure you have a study guide for each individual. You will also want to have a Bible and extra pens and pencils for group members who may have forgotten to bring one.

   **OPTION:** Personally distribute the study guides several days before this first session. Ask group members to read the introductory material in the study guide to lay the groundwork for the study.

# STARTING THE FIRST SESSION

1. Start the session on time, even if everyone is not there yet.
2. Briefly share a few positive feelings about leading this study:

   - Express your interest in strengthening your own marriage.
   - Admit that your marriage is not perfect.
   - State that the concepts in this study have been helpful in your marriage.
   - Recognize that various individuals or couples may have been reluctant to come (pressured by spouse or friend, wary of a "Christian" group, sensitive about problems with marriage, stress in schedule that makes it difficult to set aside the time for this series, etc.).
   - Thank group members for their interest and willingness to participate.

3. Hand out the study guides if you haven't already done so, and give a quick overview of The HomeBuilders Couples Series and the study guide. Briskly leaf through the study guide and point out three or four topics and the benefits of studying them. Don't be afraid of doing a little selling here—people need to know how they personally are going to profit from the study. They also need to know where this series will take them, especially if they are even a little bit apprehensive about the group.
4. Explain the format for each session in no more than two or three minutes, using Session One as your example. Each session contains the following components:

## *Focus*
A capsule statement of the main point of the session.

## *Warm Up*
A time to get better acquainted with each other and to begin thinking of the session topic.

## Blueprints

Discovering God's purposes and plans for marriage.

### HOMEBUILDERS PRINCIPLES

Summary points made throughout the study.

## Construction

Applying something that was learned, usually working as a couple.

## Make a Date

A time to decide when during the week they will complete the **HomeBuilders Project**.

### HOMEBUILDERS PROJECT

An hour during the week when husband and wife interact with the implications of what was learned. These times are really the heart of the series.

## Recommended Reading

Books that couples can read together to get maximum benefit from the study.

5. Call attention to the "ground rules" for the sessions:
   a. Share nothing about your marriage which will embarrass your mate.
   b. You may "pass" on any question you do not want to answer.
   c. Complete the **HomeBuilders Project** (questions for each couple to discuss and act on) between each session. Share one result at the next group meeting.

> **NOTE:** Beginning with the **Warm Up**, material that appears in the study guide is presented in regular type and added material for the leader appears in *italics*.

Defeating selfishness and isolation
is essential in building oneness
and a godly marriage.

*(25-40 minutes)*

*The tone for the study is set in these opening minutes, so take a good deal of time helping everyone relax and open up with each other. More serious items which come later will not be seen as threatening once people know each other and develop a measure of transparency within the group.*

*Start the sharing by explaining that one of the purposes of the study is to help everyone enjoy being together and to learn from one another's experiences. Begin by telling about incidents from your own marriage. It might be a good idea to have the spouse who is not leading the session tell these stories.*

List below the names of the couples in your group and something unique to help you remember them.

*TIP: To help get this started, each couple will be allowed up to five minutes (assign a timekeeper) to share three incidents: where and when you met; one fun or unique date before your marriage; and one humorous or romantic time from your honeymoon or early married life.*

*Set a tone of openness by sharing at a personal level, giving enough detail and color to make the stories come alive. Avoid being too reserved. Remember, your example will set the tone for honesty, humor and length.*

*Instruct each couple to take three minutes to meet together to decide what incidents they want to share and who will do the talking. Suggest that in most marriages there is a "storyteller" and a "news reporter." The news reporter is the one who just gives the bare facts. The storyteller is the one who gives the detail and color. Ask that the "storyteller" partner be the one to share. Warn them again not to share anything that would embarrass their mates.*

*Explain that as each couple shares, everyone is to write the names of the couple and one word or phrase which refers to an interesting incident about them. Ask for a couple to volunteer to go first, introducing themselves and then telling their stories. Keep the speakers to the time limit so the sharing does not drag.*

*Conclude the sharing by once again explaining the purpose of the Blueprints section. If you have more than 5 couples or less than 90 minutes for your study, reduce the time for each couple to share.*

## *Blueprints*

### *(20-30 minutes)*

*The purpose of the questions in this first part of the **Blueprints** is to go below the symptoms to discover that selfishness is the root cause that divides people.*

*One caution is appropriate here before you move your group into this discussion: this **Blueprints** section talks about selfishness and can become a negative discussion. Be sure to keep your* *group moving through this section and get them to the solution found in the first **Construction** project and the discussion that follows. The purpose of starting with the problem is to get to the root cause of mediocre marriages today and to create a need for the solution presented at the conclusion of this study.*

# A. A CAUSE OF FAILURE IN MARRIAGE
*(10-15 Minutes)*

No one starts out intending to fail in a marriage, but many do. Many homes are being built, but increasingly it seems that few succeed at building a godly marriage.

**1.** Why do you think couples are so naturally close during dating—and then often so distant after they marry?

*POSSIBLE ANSWER: Things that initially attract you to your mate may end up irritating you after you become more familiar with each other. Differences between you and your mate become magnified. Couples often work harder to please each other and to open up to each other during courtship than they do after they are married.*

*TIP: Encourage people to write down the ideas shared, since they may want to come back to certain points as they work through the **HomeBuilders Project** before the next session. Ask everyone to think for a moment of the enjoyable experiences they told about earlier and then to consider the study guide statement about failure in marriage. Point out that while everyone knows about the failure of marriages that end in divorce, many other couples continue to live together, enduring an emotional divorce.*

**2.** One of the main reasons people get married is to find intimacy—a close, personal relationship with another person. Yet it does not seem to come naturally. Why do you think this is true?

*POSSIBLE ANSWER: One common problem is selfishness—both partners going in their own directions and wanting things their own way.*

**3.** What do you see in Isaiah 53:6a which would explain the failure to achieve intimacy in marriage?

*ANSWER: "...going your own way," which is selfishness.*

*TIP: Comment that many passages dealing with the broader issues of problems in human living can provide us with clues about the cause of marital problems.*

**4.** It is easier to see selfishness in your mate than in yourself. What are some of the ways you struggle with selfishness in your marriage? List at least three.

*TIP: Share your own responses to the question first. Instruct everyone to take two or three minutes alone to list ways in which he or she struggles with selfishness. Alert them that you will ask everyone to share one item from their list. When the time is up, start with the person on your left and have everyone share one area of selfishness he or she recognizes in him- or herself.*

# B. RESULTS OF GOING YOUR OWN WAY
*(10-15 Minutes)*

**1.** How have the above examples of "going your own way" affected your marriage? Be specific.

> *TIP:* *If some people share very vague answers, i.e., "It caused problems," encourage them to think of specific evidences they noticed: attitudes, actions, communication, etc.*
>
> *Also, if some people assert that it is not wrong to look out for themselves—that they have the right to do some things that they want ("I work hard all week and deserve a chance to..."), avoid trying to label that activity as good or bad. Just rephrase Question 1: "How has that activity affected your marriage? Has it helped build intimacy with your mate, or has it created distance?"*

**2.** Selfishness in a relationship leads to isolation. (Instead of the closeness we want, we end up being separated or set apart from each other.)

`i-so-`la-tion (n) The condition of being alone, separated, solitary, set apart (from the Latin *insulatus,* made into an island). (*The American Heritage Dictionary*)

Why is isolation to be feared in marriage?

> *POSSIBLE ANSWER:* *Isolation is the opposite of intimacy and oneness. Isolation involves building walls of separation rather than bridges of communication. Isolation results in misunderstanding, pride, frustration, sexual and emotional dissatisfaction and all the other symptoms of a troubled marriage.*

*TIP: Point out that isolation is not just found in trou-bled marriages. It exists to a greater or lesser degree in every relationship where people "go their own way."*

**3.** Even stronger than fear of isolation from one's mate is the fear of being rejected by him or her. Why do you think this is so? Why are people willing to tolerate isolation, rather than working to build oneness and harmony in marriage?

The above issues lead us to consider these questions:

■ How can a couple defeat selfishness and thus avoid being isolated from one another?
■ How can a couple build a home that will withstand the pressures that are destroying marriages today?

The answer is found in a story Jesus told about two attempts to build a home.

*TIP: Invite group members to think silently for a moment about the two questions at the bottom of the study guide page.*

# *Construction*

(to be completed as a couple)
*(5-10 minutes)*

*COMMENT: This first Construction project is designed to help couples recognize that the solution to isolation in their marriages is to be committed to hearing and obeying the biblical blueprints for marriage. The storms in this story can be compared to the problems that arise in a marriage as a result of selfishness and isolation. This parable does not deal specifically with selfishness, but it does lay the essential foundation for approaching the biblical teachings on the subject.*

With your mate, read Jesus' story in Matthew 7:24-27 and complete the following chart:

| What were the two foundations? | |
|---|---|
| *Rock* | *Sand* |
| **How were the two men described?** | |
| *Wise* | *Foolish* |
| **Both men heard Christ's words; what was each man's response?** | |
| *The wise man is compared to those who act on what Christ says.* | *The foolish man is compared to those who do not.* |
| **What was the ultimate result?** | |
| *The wise man's house stood through the storm.* | *The foolish man's house was destroyed.* |

As a couple, decide which of these statements comes closest to matching your response to this story:

  □ It's a nice story, but we don't see how it fits our marriage.
  □ We get the point about putting good advice into practice, but we're not convinced Christ's advice is best.
  □ We think a lot of what Jesus said is helpful and we'll consider it.
  □ We're willing to follow Christ's teachings in our marriage.
  □ We enthusiastically embrace Christ's teachings in our marriage.

Summarize the point this story makes for your life and marriage.

*(10 minutes)*

## C. THE HOPE FOR DEFEATING SELFISHNESS AND ISOLATION *(10 Minutes)*

---

**HOMEBUILDERS PRINCIPLE #1:**

**It is only as you yield and submit your life to God, obey His Word and deny yourself that you can experience intimacy and build a godly marriage.**

---

**1.** If success in life—and marriage—rests on doing what Christ said, read the following Scriptures and discover what He said about defeating selfishness.

John 12:24,25

*ANSWER: It is necessary to die to our own desires in order to find the key to real living.*

Luke 14:27-30

*ANSWER: It is necessary to consider the cost in a relationship and to be willing to pay what it takes to make the relationship work well.*

Mark 10:43-45

> **ANSWER:** *It is necessary to serve in order to build anything great.*

**2.** How do these three statements by Christ apply to defeating selfishness and isolation in marriage? In **your** marriage?

> **TIP:** *Share some practical ways you've used those principles in your marriage.*

**3.** To pay the price, to die to self and to serve your mate— these are hard things to do. Read John 6:60,61,66-69 to find two different responses to Jesus' teachings. Summarize the two responses in the boxes below:

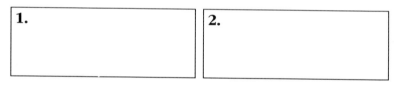

| 1. | 2. |
|---|---|
|   |   |

> **ANSWER:** *Many questioned, grumbled and decided not to follow Jesus. But Peter affirmed his belief that Jesus spoke words of life.*

Which response is closest to your reaction to Jesus' instructions about defeating selfishness?

> **TIP:** *It is likely that people in the group are struggling with some of the truths in this session. Assure them you have also had times of questioning, but encourage them to follow Peter's example. Stress the value of keeping themselves open to discovering that following Jesus' teaching is truly a great way to find real life and fulfillment in marriage.*

**4.** What point from this session do you need to obey in your marriage? What do you need to do?

*TIP: Ask group members to write their answers down and then share what they have written.*

**5.** Living in victory over selfishness is a lifelong process. A husband or wife needs the guidance of God's Word. In the passage below, underline the three building blocks which produce solid benefits in a home.

By wisdom a house is built,
and by understanding it is established;
and by knowledge the rooms are filled
with all precious and pleasant riches.
Proverbs 24:3,4

*ANSWER: Wisdom, understanding, knowledge.*

*TIP: Be certain that this session ends on a positive note. People do need to know that there is hope.*

Scripture provides the raw materials, the building blocks that we need to build a marriage marked by oneness and harmony instead of isolation. The next six sessions of this first study will explore the blueprints found in God's Word for building your home. Your discovery and application of these truths will result in a home that is built and filled ("established") with **all** precious and pleasant riches!

Make a date with your mate to meet in the next few days to complete **HomeBuilders Project #1**. Your leader will ask at the next session for you to share one thing from this experience.

_____    _____    _____
Date            Time             Location

**COMMENTS:** _Ask each couple to look at the_ **Make a Date** _section of the study guide, and to agree on a time this week to complete_ **HomeBuilders Project #1** _together. Encourage them to set aside 45 minutes to an hour to respond to the items individually and discuss their answers together._

_Each_ **HomeBuilders Project** _is absolutely essential for couples to do together during the week. Emphasize that this is not homework to earn a passing grade, but a highly significant time of interaction that will improve communication and understanding as you build your marriage according to God's blueprints._

_Point out that the questions start out fairly nonthreatening, but quickly focus on potentially sensitive issues. The intention is not to start arguments, but to stimulate honest reflection and interaction. While not every question will affect every couple in the same way, the time spent thinking and talking will be more than worthwhile for any couple._

_Remind the group that at the next session you will ask each couple to share one thing they discovered or discussed during the_ **HomeBuilders Project**. _Also, remind group members to bring their calendars to the next session as an aid in scheduling their next date with their mates._

**OPTION:** _You may want to pair each couple with another couple with whom they will agree to be accountable to complete the_ **HomeBuilders Projects**. _Have the couples tell each other when they will be doing the projects. The couples can then call each other later to see how the projects went, or you can have_ *them meet with each other for a few minutes at the start of the next session.*

*Remind everyone to help their mates this week in carrying out their planned step to overcome selfishness and isolation.*

## Recommended Reading

*COMMENTS: Call attention to the **Recommended Reading** section. The books listed at the end of each session are not required, but are recommended to reinforce and expand the concepts dealt with in the group session. Encourage couples to locate this book and read the featured chapters before the next session. One effective idea is for one spouse to read aloud to the other, either in the morning before going to work or in the evening before going to sleep.*

**Staying Close**, by Dennis Rainey.

This book by the director of FamilyLife expands on the subjects covered in this study and in our FamilyLife Marriage Conference. Chapters 1-3 will help you consider further the issues discussed in this session.

*Lead the group in a closing prayer. If you know the group members well enough, you may feel comfortable having them spend a few minutes praying for one another's intentions to overcome selfishness and isolation in the coming week.*

*Provide light refreshments and invite couples to linger and chat with each other. Informal opportunities to build relationships are a key ingredient in the success of this series. If necessary, shorten the study time in this session so that people do not feel exhausted or pressed to leave quickly.*

## HOMEBUILDERS PROJECT #1

### As a Couple: 5-10 minutes

Complete any activity from the first session that you may not have had time to complete or want to study further. Share what was most meaningful to you in Session One.

## Individually: 15-20 minutes

Write your answers to these questions.

**1.** Recall some moments during the past year when you felt close to your mate.

**2.** During those times, how was selfishness defeated?

**3.** Read John 12:24,25; Luke 14:27-30; and Mark 10:43-45. Finish this sentence: When I'm being selfish, I need to...

**4.** Read 1 Peter 3:8-12. List things you should do when your mate is being selfish:

**5.** What one thing will you do this week to show an unselfish attitude toward your mate and obey the words of Christ?

## Interact as a Couple: 25-30 minutes

**1.** Share your answers to the above questions and the discoveries that you made in answering them.

**2.** Discuss and answer the following:

No one enjoys being told that he or she is being selfish. Your marriage can benefit by knowing how to approach one another when the other mate is being selfish. Wisdom, gentleness and a proper approach can all help bring the selfish one back to a correct perspective. Share a couple of ways your mate could **help you** deal with your selfishness:

(It would be a good idea to get your mate's "permission" before applying these suggestions.)

**3.** Agree on any action you will take.

**4.** Close your time together by praying for one another.

Remember to bring your calendar for **Make a Date**
to the next session.

# CREATING ONENESS

## OBJECTIVES

You will help your group members nurture oneness in their marriages as you guide them to:

- Discover the benefits of oneness in marriage;
- Identify commitment to God's blueprints as the key to achieving oneness and harmony in marriage;
- Evaluate how God's blueprints for marriage are being followed in their homes; and
- Plan specific ways in which to mirror God's image better in their marriages.

## OVERALL COMMENTS

1. Session One focused on problems in a marriage. This session is the first to begin exploring God's blueprints for the solution to selfishness and isolation. Be sensitive to those individuals or couples who struggle with accepting God's purposes as their own. Your warmth and acceptance can have a significant role in someone's becoming willing to really consider the principles of these sessions.
2. You may wish to have extra study guides and Bibles for any who did not bring theirs.
3. Again, light refreshments as people arrive help set a tone of friendly anticipation. And many would find name tags helpful.
4. If someone joins the group for the first time at this session,

give a summary of the main thrust of Session One as people are gathering. Also, be sure to introduce those who do not know each other and assist them in beginning some informal conversation. You may wish to start a little early and have each new couple complete the **Warm Up** from Session One.

# *Focus*

Oneness in marriage is achieved as both husband and wife yield to God and work together in building their home from the same set of blueprints: the Bible.

# *Warm Up*

*(15-25 minutes)*

**COMMENT:** *Ask for a show of hands of those who completed the **HomeBuilders Project** from the last session. Do not chide those who did not, but encourage them to complete this week's project and, if needed, make up last week's unfinished projects. Have two people share one result or insight from their project (the purpose of this is for accountability). Congratulate those who did the project, and underscore the importance of doing the project from each session.*

**1.** What was the most meaningful result of the last session as you worked with your mate to overcome selfishness and isolation? What have you discovered about yourself and your mate?

*TIP: Share with the group your answer. Let the group discuss their own answers, but don't force it—keep it moving. Summarize this sharing by calling attention to the Session One review statement in the study guide.*

In the first session, you saw that selfishness produces isolation in marriage. Neither is a part of God's plan for marriage—instead, He wants to defeat them. Let's look at His blueprint for replacing isolation (a natural result) with oneness (a supernatural result).

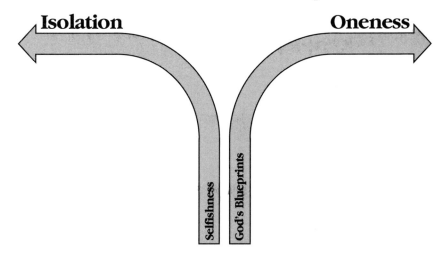

**Isolation** **Oneness**

Selfishness    God's Blueprints

*OPTIONAL WARM UP: If you sense that the people in your group could use something to help them relax and regain feelings of openness, the following game can help. It is planned to allow people to work together at a task, helping them feel positive about others in the group.*

*Divide the group into two teams: men versus women! Explain the game thoroughly before starting.*

*You will need the following for the game:*

- *Two pads of 8 ½ x 11-inch paper and two pencils (one pad and pencil for each group);*
- *Two areas that have a flat surface (table) that a group of four to seven adults can gather around;*
- *Three lists of the same words on separate sheets of paper;*

■ *A place to stand that is equal in distance from both groups and is clear for people to run back and forth from their group (this game can and should get lively).*

*The game is "Paper Charades." Each team will send one representative to you to start the game. You will show representatives the first item on your list of words. They will then return to their teams and draw a picture to lead their teams to guess the word. The person drawing the picture (representative) cannot speak any words or make any sounds. As soon as a team guesses correctly, another team member will come to you, tell you the correct word and get the next word. The first team to guess all the words on the list is the winner and should be rewarded appropriately (perhaps by having the losers prepare and serve refreshments at the next session).*

*Be sure to cover your list until the person has given you the correct word. Then point to the next word in the list, keeping the remaining words covered. Use the following words as time allows, making sure you start with those on List 1, move on to List 2 and conclude with List 3. Explain that the first two lists each contain 10 simple words and will be completed rather fast, so speed is the key to victory. The third list, you should explain, is much harder because it is made up of concepts and thus will take longer. Be aware of your time limit as the third list will go very slowly. You may wish to set a time limit before starting the third list.*

| **List 1** *Simple Objects* | **List 2** *Simple Objects* | **List 3** *Concepts (much harder)* |
|---|---|---|
| *hammer* | *roof* | *harmony* |
| *ladder* | *toilet* | *intimacy* |
| *couch* | *carpet* | *memories* |
| *lamp* | *foundation* | *honeymoon* |
| *mailbox* | *blueprints* | *romance* |
| *shovel* | *nails* | |
| *toolbox* | *bulldozer* | |
| *television* | *porch* | |
| *piano* | *carpenter* | |
| *bathtub* | *window* | |

*When you finish the game, ask the groups what all the words had in common. Most likely, they have already noticed that all the words had something to do with building a house.*

*(30-40 minutes)*

*Point out that it is easy to see the benefit of oneness or unity in a physical activity such as a three-legged race or a tug-of-war. Marriage, however, is a very complex relationship, and the effort required to defeat selfishness and achieve oneness may sometimes seem too steep a price to pay. This **Blueprints** section will look at a few of the many rich benefits that oneness provides which really do make the process of defeating selfishness more than worthwhile.*

## A. THE BENEFITS OF ONENESS *(10 minutes)*

**1.** What do the following Scriptures teach us about some of the benefits of oneness in a relationship?

Psalm 133:1

> **ANSWER:** *Pleasant...living in unity.*

Ecclesiastes 4:9-12

> **ANSWER:** *Helping in labor. Assisting one who falls. Warmth. Strength against adversaries.*

**2.** From your experience, what are some other benefits you gain from being one with your mate?

*TIP: Divide the group into same-sex partners. Then have each pair work together in writing a list of other benefits of being one with our mate. Allow about two minutes, then call for volunteers to read aloud items from their lists.*

*State that knowing the benefits of oneness leads to an obvious question: How do we achieve it in our marriage? Answering this question is the focus of the next segment.*

---

**HOMEBUILDERS PRINCIPLE #2:**

## Oneness in marriage involves complete unity with each other.

---

# B. ACHIEVING ONENESS *(10-15 minutes)*

**1.** What would society say is the way to achieve oneness in marriage?

*ANSWER: By working hard at your marriage. By improving your sex life. By each of you doing your share in household responsibilities and in working on the relationship (the 50/50 plan).*

*TIP: Point out that at least some of the ideas shared are very positive, helpful suggestions. However, most human plans tend to miss some very important factors.*

**2.** What important factors are missing from most secular instruction in achieving oneness?

*ANSWER: Involving God in a relationship. Obedience to God's Word. Recognition of selfishness as the root cause of trouble and solving it as a problem. Awareness that only God offers the means to change a selfish nature.*

**3.** In his letter to the church at Philippi, Paul addressed the issue of oneness among Christians. The points he made also show how to achieve oneness within marriage.

1 "If therefore there is any encouragement in Christ, if there is any consolation of love, if there is any fellowship of the Spirit, if any affection and compassion,
2 make my joy complete by being of the same mind, maintaining the same love, united in spirit, intent on one purpose.
3 Do nothing from selfishness or empty conceit, but with humility of mind let each of you regard one another as more important than himself;
4 do not merely look out for your own personal interests, but also for the interests of others."

Philippians 2:1-4

*TIP: Call on a volunteer to read aloud the introductory statement under Item 3. Then ask four other people to each read aloud one verse of Philippians 2:1-4.*

What does Paul say in verses 3 and 4 that relates to what you learned from Session One about selfishness?

*ANSWER: Don't act from selfishness, have a humble attitude and put the interests and needs of others ahead of our own.*

**4.** Share an illustration of a time when you did or did not deny yourself for your mate:

What was the result?

> **TIP:** *Briefly share an illustration of one time when you did or did not deny yourself for your mate. Then invite others in the group to tell of a similar incident. Ask the others in the group to tell the result in their marriage of incidents when they did not deny themselves.*

> **OPTION:** *If time allows, call attention to verse 1, pointing out that the repeated word "if" is not an expression of doubt, but is a literary device used for emphasis. Other ways of phrasing include "since" or "because" or "obviously there is." Ask, "What does verse 1 indicate about the foundation on which oneness is built?"*

**5.** What does verse 2 say to you about how to achieve oneness in a relationship?

> **TIP:** *Be sure the group recognizes the emphasis Paul is placing on oneness by defining it with four distinct phrases: "being of the same mind, maintaining the same love, united in spirit, intent on one purpose."*
>
> *Point out that Paul's phrase, "intent on one purpose," leads us to examine what God's purpose—or blueprint—for marriage really is.*

> **OPTION:** *You may want to share this four-step plan for achieving oneness:*
> *1. Agree on the goal.*
> *2. Deal with any conflict.*
> *3. Walk together.*
> *4. Build from the same set of blueprints.*

---

**HOMEBUILDERS PRINCIPLE #3:**

In order to achieve oneness, a couple must share a strong commitment to God's purpose for marriage.

---

# C. GOD'S PURPOSE FOR MARRIAGE

*(10-15 minutes)*

**1.** Match the following Scriptures with God's five purposes for marriage:

| | |
|---|---|
| a. Genesis 1:26,27 | MANAGE God's Creation |
| b. Genesis 1:28a | MODEL Christ's Relationship to His Church |
| c. Genesis 1:28b | MIRROR God's Image |
| d. Genesis 2:18 & 1 Corinthians 11:11 | MULTIPLY a Godly Heritage |
| e. Ephesians 5:31 | MUTUALLY Complete One Another |

*ANSWER:*
*a. Genesis 1:26,27*    *MIRROR God's Image* ✓
*b. Genesis 1:28a*    *MULTIPLY a Godly Heritage* ✓
*c. Genesis 1:28b*    *MANAGE God's Creation* ✓
*d. Genesis 2:18 &*    *MUTUALLY Complete One Another* ✓
*   1 Corinthians 11:11*
*e. Ephesians 5:31*    *MODEL Christ and Church* ✓

**TIP:** *Assign each couple one of the Scriptures listed and instruct them to match that Scripture with the appropriate statement defining part of God's blueprints for marriage. Allow two or three minutes for couples to read and discuss. If some couples finish before others, suggest that they read one or more of the other Scriptures.*

**2.** Why is each purpose important in a marriage? List ways each can be applied in your marriage today.

*ANSWER:*

    *MIRROR God's Image: Both male and female were created in God's image. Both have equal dignity and with it equal responsibility to live as God's person in the home and community.*

    *MULTIPLY a Godly Heritage: Marriage is not just for the benefit of the couple, but is to produce others who reflect God in the world.*

    *MANAGE God's Creation: All that a couple does should be evaluated in light of the responsibility of being good stewards of all God has provided.*

    *MUTUALLY Complete One Another: Each person is incomplete; marriage is God's best means for filling the gaps as each person is made whole by meeting the needs of the other.*

    *MODEL Christ and the Church: The unselfish love of a husband and the willing submission of a wife is a living example of the relationship between Christ and His church.*

---

**HOMEBUILDERS PRINCIPLE #4:**

## When we yield to God and build together from His blueprints, we begin the process of experiencing oneness.

---

# Construction

(to be completed as a couple)
*(15-25 minutes)*

*This **Construction** project helps a couple evaluate how they are doing in mirroring God's image in various areas of their lives. This awareness is intended to lead a couple to identify at least one specific way in which they can grow in fulfilling God's purpose for their marriage.*

*Instruct each couple to find a comfortable spot and work together to complete the five items in the **Construction** section. State how much time you will allow (at least eight minutes) and that you will monitor the time so they can keep moving and complete all five items. They may want to go back to some of the items later in the week for a more thorough consideration. Explain that you will ask each couple to share one item from this section. Before they begin work, share your own completion of one line on the chart as a sample of how they might proceed with the first item. Be willing to show your imperfections and your desire to grow so that others may feel able to respond honestly to these probing questions.*

Let's consider one of the five purposes for marriage:

**1.** How well is your marriage mirroring God's image—representing Him—in the areas and relationships listed below? **Rate yourselves on a scale of 1 (lowest) to 10 (highest) in how your marriage reflects God to these people:**

| We mirror God's | to each other | to our children | to our neighbors | to coworkers |
|---|---|---|---|---|
| ...perfect love for imperfect people; | | | | |
| ...commitment by patient support; | | | | |
| ...loving-kindness, by serving to meet needs; | | | | |
| ...peace, by resolving conflicts. | | | | |

**2.** Are there any hindrances to your mirroring God's image in your marriage? Discuss with each other what needs to be done to remove any barriers.

**3.** What did you learn about your marriage from this evaluation?

*As couples work, announce two or three times how much time they have left and approximately how far they should be by this point. Also be available to answer questions in case anyone is uncertain of how to proceed with an item.*

*Call time and invite each couple to share their answer to one item they discussed. You may want to begin the sharing yourself.*

*Ask everyone to look at the **Make a Date** section of the study guide and to take a moment to agree with their mate on a time this week to complete the **HomeBuilders Project**. Remind them that at the next session you will ask them to share one experience from this interaction.*

---

Make a date with your mate to meet in the next few days to complete **HomeBuilders Project #2**. Your leader will ask at the next session for you to share one thing from this experience.

_____ _____ _____
Date          Time          Location

---

# Recommended Reading

**Staying Close**, by Dennis Rainey.
Chapters 11 and 12—"God's Purpose for Oneness" and "The Master Plan for Oneness"—expand on the material discussed in this session.

*Dismiss in prayer, or invite group members to volunteer one-sentence prayers asking God's help in creating true oneness in marriage.*
*Invite everyone to enjoy a time of refreshments and fellowship.*

## HOMEBUILDERS PROJECT #2

### As a Couple: 5-10 minutes
Review Session Two and complete any previous sessions and/or projects that are not finished. Discuss those points that stand out in your mind.

### Individually: 15-20 minutes
Answer each of the following questions and prepare to discuss them with your mate.

**1.** What would our closest friends say is the purpose of our marriage?

**2.** In which of God's purposes are we succeeding? (Manage, model, mirror, multiply, mutually complete.)

**3.** Which ones need work in our marriage? In what way?

**4.** What hinders our success in accomplishing these purposes?

**5.** What tough decisions need to be made **now**? In the next 6 to 12 months?

**6.** What one step could we take this week to move toward fulfilling one of God's purposes in our marriage?

## Interact as a Couple: 25-30 minutes

Discuss with your mate your reflections on and discoveries from the above questions. Please be sure to **agree** on any action step and **how** it will be implemented. Close your time together by praying for one another and for your success in fulfilling God's purposes for your marriage.

Remember to bring your calendar for **Make a Date** to the next session.

# RECEIVING YOUR MATE

## OBJECTIVES

You will help your group members nurture oneness in their marriages as you guide them to:

- Identify the ways Adam needed Eve and compare those with ways they need their mates;
- Discuss the importance and the basis of receiving their mates as God's perfect provision;
- Analyze how weaknesses in mates have an impact on receiving them as God's provision; and
- Affirm specific ways they and their mates need each other and can accept one another as God's gift.

## OVERALL COMMENTS

1. By the third session your group members should have come to know one another well enough to feel somewhat relaxed and comfortable in talking with each other—at least about external aspects of their marriages. This session probes some very sensitive areas, exploring ways that we need our mates. Some people may have difficulty admitting these ways to themselves or to their mates, let alone to other people. Your role here, providing acceptance and support without pressing anyone, is crucial. Pray for sensitivity to each person as a unique being. And remind people that they can pass on any question they prefer not to answer.

2. The **Warm Up** questions are important not only to remind people of earlier content, but to establish a sense of mutual accountability. If your group members merely come to seven meetings and do not build a commitment to follow through with genuine growth efforts, they will gain little from this study.

## Focus

Oneness in marriage requires receiving your mate as God's perfect provision for your needs.

## Warm Up
*(10-20 minutes)*

*This **Warm Up** section builds on the mutual trust and concern that has been built in your group during the first two sessions. The questions encourage people to reveal a little more of themselves, helping them develop honest and open responses to the questions which follow.*

***OPTION:*** *Because some people feel uncomfortable sharing in a mixed group, you may want to have people discuss the three **Warm Up** questions in separate groups of men and women. Have one group move to another room if possible, with you and your spouse each leading one group's discussion. Smaller groups will also allow more people to share within the time available. But if your group is finding it easy to share openly, consider keeping the entire group together. If you do break up into two groups, and if time allows, have each person share an answer to one item when the two groups come together.*

**1.** One thing I **would not** want to change about my mate is...

**2.** What are your mate's three greatest strengths—and how do they complement your own strengths and weaknesses?*

> *TIP: Tell the group about your own mate's greatest strengths and how you feel they complement your strengths and weaknesses. Then ask each person to share his response to Item 2.*

**3.** Share your answer to one of these questions from **Home-Builders Project #2**:

☐ What would your closest friends say is the purpose of your marriage?

☐ What one step did you take since our last session toward fulfilling one of God's purposes in your marriage?

> *TIP: Ask for a show of hands of those who completed **HomeBuilders Project #2**. Commend those who did it and stress the long-term value of regularly setting aside time with our mates to talk about our relationship. Share your answer to one of the two **Home-Builders Project** questions, then ask your group members to share their answers to one of the questions.*

*Questions taken from *The Questions Book for Marriage Intimacy* by Dennis and Barbara Rainey. Published by FamilyLife, 1988.

We have seen that selfishness produces isolation in marriage, while following God's blueprints leads to oneness. Now we will explore the importance of receiving one's mate as God's special gift for our aloneness needs.

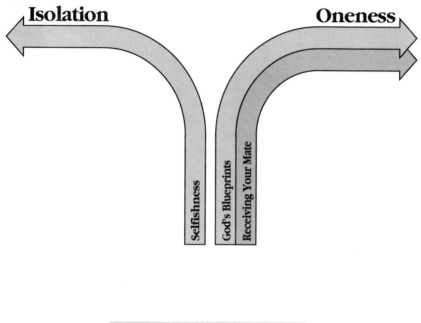

### Blueprints

*(35-50 minutes)*

*The **Blueprints** section explores a key principle: The joy of God's provision. Many couples do not understand this principle and thereby miss out on it. This study helps each individual recognize areas of personal need and accept his or her mate as God's provision for those needs.*

In Genesis 2:18-23, we find the familiar story of Adam and Eve. Our familiarity with Scriptures such as this can blind us to profound insights—insights that, when applied, can strengthen every marriage. Let's look at what we can learn from this passage to help us achieve oneness in marriage:

# A. EVERYONE'S NEED (GENESIS 2:18)
*(5-10 minutes)*

**1.** What need did God build into Adam that was not filled by God's personal presence? What was "not good" about Adam as God created him?

> ***ANSWER:*** *Adam needed a mate, a companion, "a helper suitable for him" or "corresponding to him." "Alone" in this context is obviously a negative situation, since God specifically said it was "not good" and took action to remedy the problem.*

> ***TIP:*** *To help your group members focus on what was negative in the situation, you may want to ask a follow-up question such as, "What is another word for being alone?" (Isolation.)*

**2.** What are some likely reasons why God made Adam incomplete?

> ***ANSWER:*** *To keep him from feeling self-sufficient. To enable him to recognize his need of God and of his mate, so that his mate would be able to provide for areas in which he lacked.*

**3.** Identify two or three ways you are incomplete and need your mate.

> ***TIP:*** *Your group members may not be accustomed to thinking in these terms. To get them started, share some ways that you are incomplete without your mate. Another idea would be to ask each person to*

*work privately to respond to Item 3 and be ready to share one answer with the group. After two or three minutes, ask all group members to tell one way they need their mates.*

# B. AWARENESS OF NEED (GENESIS 2:19,20) *(10-15 minutes)*

**1.** What did naming animals have to do with Adam's aloneness? How aware of being alone do you think Adam was before he named the animals?

*ANSWER: Adam recognized that he did not have a suitable companion. There is no evidence Adam had any awareness of his need before then.*

*TIP: Read aloud verses 19 and 20 of Genesis 2.*

**2.** Why did God want Adam to see his need for a mate?

*ANSWER: Until Adam recognized his need, he would never adequately appreciate God or God's provision, Eve.*

*TIP: Point out that while it may be fun to speculate about what went on in Adam's head, we must not lose sight of what God was trying to do. Ask for several people to share their responses to the question.*

**3.** What are some ways you see your need for your mate today that you did not recognize when you first got married?

**4.** How do you think your awareness of needing your mate may change in the next five years?

> *TIP: If responses are slow in coming, ask, "If things continue as they are now, do you think in five years you will be more aware of your need for your mate or less aware?" You might suggest this as a question for couples to refer back to while working on the Home-Builders Project this week.*

**5.** At the beginning of your relationship with your mate, how aware was God of all your needs (past, present and future)?

> *ANSWER: He was completely aware of your needs. Your mate is God's provision for your needs.*

> *TIP: This is a key point for couples to digest. Many married couples end up spending so much time focusing on their mate's shortcomings that they forget how much they need their mates. And the thought that God actually gave their mates to them to meet their needs may strike some couples as incredible. If you sense that couples don't grasp the significance of this fact, you might turn to your mate and say something like, "God gave me this person in order to meet my needs. She is God's provision for me." Invite them to consider the fact that the same is true for them.*

## C. GOD'S PROVISION FOR OUR NEED (GENESIS 2:21,22) *(10 minutes)*

**1.** List five things God did in these verses:

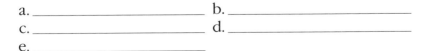

a. _____ b. _____

c. _____ d. _____

e. _____

*ANSWER: Caused Adam to sleep; took a rib; closed the flesh; made a woman; and brought her to Adam.*

*TIP: Guide the group in listing God's five actions described in Genesis 2:21,22.*

**2.** Which of these actions seems most significant to you? Why?

*ANSWER:*
*Caused Adam to sleep: Besides making the following surgical procedure easier, some people speculate that this step kept Adam from offering unwanted advice on the woman's design.*

*Took a rib: This implies God recognized the equality of woman with man, as well as depicting the strong emotional bonds between the sexes.*

*Closed the flesh: Adam was not harmed by this endeavor.*

*Made a woman: She was totally God's handiwork.*

*Brought her to Adam: God is obviously concerned about Adam's response to the woman and wanted her to be recognized as coming from Him. Since this is the only step in the process that Adam was able to observe, it was an act that had great impact upon him.*

# D. OUR RESPONSE TO GOD'S PROVISION (GENESIS 2:23) *(10-15 minutes)*

**1.** What had Eve done up to this point to warrant Adam's acceptance?

*ANSWER: Other than obviously looking better to*

*Adam than any of the animals he had been naming, she had done nothing. Nor had he done anything to earn acceptance from her.*

**2.** Why was Adam able to immediately recognize Eve as the mate who would fulfill his need?

> **ANSWER:** *We can assume there was an immediate attraction between them. However, the only clue given in the passage is that Adam must have recognized that God was presenting her as a gift from Himself. And she knew that God had specifically brought her to Adam.*

**3.** Who did Adam know better, Eve or God?

> **ANSWER:** *Obviously, God. Why is this important? Although Adam did not yet know Eve, he did know God and trusted Him.*

**4.** Are you more a student of:

☐ your mate (strengths, weaknesses, etc.)
OR
☐ the One who provided him/her for you?

*TIP: Guide the group in considering the implications of Adam's reception of his mate for their marriages. Instruct participants to mark Question 4, indicating whether they are more a student of their mate or of God, the One who provided him/her. Comment that this passage clarifies two important concepts:*

▪ *No married person is complete until he/she is united with his/her God-given counterpart. Many individuals struggle within their marriage because they are unaware of their need of their mate.*

■ *Acceptance of our mate as God's provision for our needs frees the relationship of the pressure which results when acceptance is based on performance. Just as Eve did nothing to earn Adam's acceptance, we do not have to perform or satisfy someone's list of conditions. And like Adam, we need to receive our mate simply on the basis of Who gave him/her to us.*

---

**HOMEBUILDERS PRINCIPLE #5:**

## The basis for my acceptance of my mate is faith in God's character and trustworthiness.

---

**5.** What causes us to reject rather than receive our mate?

*TIP: Encourage people to think of specific incidents in which they reacted with rejection rather than acceptance. Summarize the ideas shared with this comment: "We tend to focus on our mate and lose our focus on God. And when we are focused on our mate, it is usually easier to notice flaws than strengths."*

**6.** Since God provided your mate, can you reject your mate without rejecting God? Why?

*ANSWER: No. Rejection of the gift is rejection of the Giver.*

*TIP: If you have non-Christians in the group or people who were not Christians when they married, ask the group to suggest an answer for someone who says, "But when we were married, neither of us even knew God, let alone trusted Him. How could my mate be God's gift to me under that circumstance?" (The Scriptures clearly show that God is sovereign in the affairs of individuals and nations. Have the group look at Romans 8:28 to see the most common way God demonstrates His sovereignty: He shows His authority by turning even what is done in rebellion against Him into results that achieve His purposes. See Genesis 50:20.)*

*If the issue of spouse abuse is raised, call attention to these Scriptures that provide wise counsel:*

*Romans 13:1 and 1 Peter 2:13-15 teach God's establishment of governmental authority to control those who do wrong. A person in danger should not hesitate to contact the authorities for protection.*

*Romans 5:8 shares Christ's example of loving the sinner even though hating sin (Psalm 45:7). One spouse's wrong acts do not excuse retaliation by the other.*

*Proverbs 14:7 says to "leave the presence of a fool." This does not mean divorce; it simply advises establishing enough space to avoid the influence of the fool.*

**7.** Consider the results of not receiving your mate. Describe such a marriage 10 to 20 years from now.

*TIP: Assign each couple to work together in completing Question 7, writing a description of a marriage after 10 to 20 years during which the partners did not receive one another. Allow 2 or 3 minutes for people to jot down a few thoughts, then call for volunteers to read their predictions. After several have been read, ask, "What do these predictions say to you about receiving your mate as God's best provision for your needs?"*

**8.** Which of these statements could you most readily apply in your marriage: Weaknesses in my mate are...

☐ a. opportunities for me to be needed.

☐ b. tools of God to cause me to trust Him.

☐ c. only changed through a climate of loving acceptance.

> *TIP: Instruct each person to mark one of the three statements on weaknesses which could most readily apply in his or her marriage. Ask for a show of hands of those who chose the first statement. Do the same for the other two. Then invite someone who marked the statement most commonly chosen to explain why he or she feels that idea is significant. After two or three have commented, do the same for the other two statements. If no one chooses a particular statement, share your own thoughts on its importance.*

---
### HOMEBUILDERS PRINCIPLE #6:

## A godly marriage is not created by finding a perfect, flawless person, but is created by allowing God's perfect love and acceptance to flow through one imperfect person—you— toward another imperfect person—your mate.
---

*TIP: Ask each person to silently read **HomeBuilders Principle #6**.*

# Construction

(to be completed as a couple)
*(15-20 minutes)*

**1.** Individually, list ways you see your mate needing you. (Try to list 10 if time permits.)

**2.** Share your list with your mate.

> **TIP:** *At the end of the allotted time, ask each person to share one item from his or her list and how the spouse reacted to that item.*

# Make a Date

Make a date with your mate to meet in the next few days to complete **HomeBuilders Project #3**. Your leader will ask at the next session for you to share one thing from this experience.

| Date | Time | Location |
| --- | --- | --- |

*Remind couples to set and keep their date to complete **Home-Builders Project #3**. Stress its value in making the truth of the session practical in their relationships. Point out which project they should do (those who have not attended the FamilyLife Marriage Conference should do #3A; FamilyLife Marriage Conference alumni should do #3B).*

# Recommended Reading

*Call attention to the* **Recommended Reading.**

**Building Your Mate's Self-Esteem**, by Dennis and Barbara Rainey.

Accepting your mate is one of the cornerstones of godly marriage. This book can help you express your acceptance and belief in each other. An intensely practical book, it will teach you how to deal with the haunting problems of the past, how to give your mate the freedom to fail and how to help your mate be liberated from questions of self-doubt.

**Staying Close**, by Dennis Rainey.

Chapters 5-7 will help you consider further the issues discussed in this session.

*Conclude with a brief time of prayer. Perhaps each person can pray aloud, thanking God for his/her mate. Invite everyone to enjoy a time of refreshments and fellowship.*

## PROJECT #3

There are two **HomeBuilders Projects** for you to choose from for this session. Project #3A is for those who have not attended a FamilyLife Marriage Conference. Project #3B is for conference alumni.

## HOMEBUILDERS PROJECT #3A

### Individually: 40 minutes

**A.** Write out the answers to the following questions in the form of a love letter. Use the page at the end of this project for your letter (30 minutes).

1. What were the qualities that attracted me the most to you when we first met?

2. Do I see and accept you as you really are? What have I not accepted in you?

3. Do you see and accept me as I really am? In what areas do I feel that you have not accepted me? How does this make me feel?

**B.** Spend time in prayer, individually (10 minutes).

1. Confess to God any rejection of, withdrawal from or bitterness toward your mate as sin. Thank God for His forgiveness and the cleansing blood of Christ.

   "If we confess our sins, He is faithful and righteous to forgive us our sins and to cleanse us from all unrighteousness" (1 John 1:9).

2. Commit to God totally, by faith, to receive your mate based upon the integrity and sovereignty of God. Be sure to put this commitment in your love letter.

3. Commit to God to trust Him with your mate's weaknesses and to love your mate unconditionally with Christ's love (apart from performance.) Be certain you put this commitment in your love letter.

## Interact as a Couple: 15-20 minutes

**1.** Share and discuss your letter.

**2.** Verbalize to your mate the commitment you made to God during your individual prayer time.

**3.** Close your time together by taking turns thanking God for each other.

Remember to bring your calendar for **Make a Date** to the next session.

# HOMEBUILDERS PROJECT #3B

## As a Couple: 5-10 minutes

Review the concept we studied in Session Three. Share what really impressed you in the study. Go back over any sections you wanted to discuss with your mate but were unable to.

## Individually: 25-30 minutes

Complete the project below. (You may need more time—that's fine. It is important to take enough time to accurately express to your mate how you feel about him/her.)

**1.** Do an inventory of the ways your mate is meeting your needs. Try to list 25 or more if you can. (List on a separate sheet of paper.)

**2.** Identify which of those are the five most important ways you need him or her.

**3.** Identify those differences in your mate that God uses to complete you.

**4.** Identify one or two areas in which you may have been rejecting or not totally accepting your mate. What has been the result of that rejection for you? For your mate?

**5.** Do you need to ask forgiveness for your lack of acceptance toward your mate? If appropriate, express this to your mate.

## Interact as a Couple: 15-20 minutes

**1.** Share the results of your project with your mate.

**2.** Affirm (or reaffirm) to your mate your acceptance of him or her as God's perfect provision for your needs.

**3.** Close your time together in prayer, thanking God for one another.

Remember to bring your calendar for **Make a Date**
to the next session.

# CONSTRUCTING
# A RELATIONSHIP

## OBJECTIVES

You will help your group members construct a distinctively Christian marriage as you guide them to:

- Define the importance of leaving their own parents;
- Evaluate the ways in which they are currently cleaving to their mates;
- Identify the connection between becoming one flesh and achieving oneness; and
- Practice demonstrating transparency with their mates.

## OVERALL COMMENTS

You will find you need to monitor time very carefully in this session because each of the four parts of the **Blueprints** section can generate a great deal of interesting interaction. The **Construction** activities can generate even more dialogue. If the group seems intent on staying with a section longer than your time allotment, point out that part of the purpose of the session is to raise issues for couples to discuss further at home. Avoid making frequent references to time limitations, but keep the group aware that the point they are dissecting is best understood in light of the total set of truths being dealt with in the session.

# Focus

The process of becoming one requires
that a couple construct their marriage
by leaving parents, cleaving to each
other and becoming one flesh.

# Warm Up

*(10-15 minutes)*

**1.** What was one of the first difficult challenges in your commitment to each other that you faced in the early years of your marriage?

**2.** How did that challenge affect your commitment to each other?

> *TIP: To encourage openness in sharing, to allow for more sharing within the available time and to make it easier in the next session when the entire time is spent in separate men's and women's groups, consider having the men and women meet separately. To add a dimension of fun, and if time allows, you might want to check stories when the groups complete their sharing and then meet together. Find out whether any couples both told of the same challenge, and if so, whether their view on it varied in any way.*

> *Ask each person to reflect on the **HomeBuilders** Project from Session Three. Ask for a show of hands of those who did the project. Do not chide those who did not, but encourage them to complete it and, if needed, make up unfinished projects. Have two people share one result of their projects (the purpose of this is for accountability). Congratulate those who did and underscore the importance of doing the project for each session.*

In Session Three we saw that with our confidence in God's character and trustworthiness, we can totally accept and receive our mate as His provision for our needs. Many couples today have yet to realize that they have not been following the biblical blueprints for becoming one. God's blueprints for the lifelong process of constructing a godly marriage have three practical phases.

# *Blueprints*

*(35-50 minutes)*

*This **Blueprints** section explores three phases in the construction of a Christian marriage. One of the most common errors is assuming that each phase has already been fulfilled. Far too many people think that the command to leave parents, cleave together and become one flesh is aimed at newlyweds. This study will show that each phase must be a lifelong process in order for a couple to achieve and maintain a relationship of openness and trust.*

## A. PHASE 1—LEAVE (GENESIS 2:24)
*(10-15 minutes)*

**1.** Once a couple has received each other as God's gift (Genesis 2:18-23), they must leave their parents. What factors are involved in "leaving" one's parents? How do people establish and maintain independence from parents?

> ***ANSWER:*** *Leaving involves physical, emotional and financial separation, transferring dependence from parents to mate.*

> ***NOTE:*** *The Hebrew term translated "leave" means "to loosen," "to relinquish," or "to forsake."*

**2.** Answer the question that fits your situation. What are some ways:

a. couples in the first few years of marriage do not leave their parents?

> ***POSSIBLE ANSWER:*** *Continuing to receive financial help. Asking parents to resolve conflicts. Frequently visiting or calling parents.*

b. couples in later years of marriage do not leave their parents?

> ***POSSIBLE ANSWER:*** *Putting parents' needs ahead of those of mate. Seeking parental advice or approval in place of mate's.*

> ***TIP:*** *If the couples in your group vary significantly in the length of time they have been married, ask each couple to answer either Question 2a or 2b, depending on which comes closest to their situation. If your couples have all been married about the same length of time, lead them all in answering either Question 2a or 2b.*

c. couples who marry later in life and do not leave parents and/or leave their independent life-style?

**3.** What can happen in a marriage when:

a. parents are "too clingy"?

> **POSSIBLE ANSWER:** *The child may not mature. The spouse may develop resentments which create conflicts.*

b. the son/daughter is dependent on parents and not on his/her mate?

> **ANSWER:** *Mate is not allowed to meet spouse's needs, thwarting oneness in the relationship.*
>
> **TIP:** *Make sure the group members recognize that no longer being dependent on parents does not mean not having a relationship with them. For example, a couple may borrow money from parents. This transaction would probably not indicate dependence on parents if it is handled in a businesslike manner with an agreed-upon plan for repayment which is then honored. Nor would parental help in a crisis necessarily indicate undue dependence. But a pattern of going to parents for repeated assistance is a serious danger signal.*

**4.** Ephesians 6:2,3 commands us, "Honor your father and mother." What are some practical ways of honoring your parents and providing for them without becoming dependent on them?

**POSSIBLE ANSWER:** *Pray for your parents. Write and call them regularly. Organize special events to honor them. Put together a special, written tribute to your parents. Care for them when your help is needed.*

*TIP:* *Direct the group to read Ephesians 6:2,3. If any couples in your group have parents who are now elderly and becoming incapable of caring for themselves, ask, "How can a couple balance responsibilities to each other with the needs of aging parents?"*

*ANSWER: One's mate must always be given first priority, but that can never be made into an excuse to neglect responsibility to parents. See Mark 7:6-13 for Jesus' accusation against those who used their religious vows as an excuse to avoid caring for their parents.*

**5.** Are there ways you and your mate have not left your parents? How?

*TIP:* *Ask each individual to take two or three minutes to write answers to Question 5. Then instruct couples to exchange study guides and spend a few more minutes discussing their answers with each other.*

**6.** What practical advice would you give to:

a. the dependent son/daughter?

b. the son/daughter whose parents are "too clingy"?

*TIP: Call on someone who has not spoken aloud for a while to offer a suggestion in response to Question 6a. Then invite several others to add further suggestions. Repeat the process with Question 6b.*

# B. PHASE 2—CLEAVE (GENESIS 2:24B)
*(10-15 minutes)*

**1.** What does the phrase "cleave to his wife" mean in this verse?

*ANSWER: The term conveys the sense of strong emotional attachments, a bonding. The Hebrew term for "cleave" involves the idea of clinging, adhering, being united. Cleaving involves a commitment—a promise, guarantee, assurance—to one another, and so involves an act of the will, a conscious decision to form a permanent bond. Thus, cleaving is both a one-time decision and an ongoing process which must be continually reaffirmed.*

*TIP: Invite a volunteer to read aloud Genesis 2:24 before asking the question.*

**2.** What is the relationship between leaving your parents and cleaving to your mate?

*ANSWER: A couple cannot fully cleave to each other until they have truly left their parents. Also, the decision to leave parents cannot be maintained unless the couple continues to cleave to one another.*

*TIP: Refer back to the discussion on leaving parents and ask Question 2.*

**3.** What factors in society and in marriage make cleaving difficult?

> ***ANSWER:*** *If people run out of ideas, ask them to think of factors within an individual (pride, selfishness, etc.), factors between partners (poor communication, competition, etc.) and factors outside the couple (job pressures, in-laws, finances, etc.).*
>
> ***TIP:*** *Ask each person to respond to Question 3, suggesting one factor in society and/or in marriage which can make cleaving difficult for a couple to do.*

**4.** Malachi 2:15b,16 says, "'Take heed, then, to your spirit, and let no one deal treacherously against the wife of your youth. For I hate divorce,' says the Lord." Why is cleaving so important to God?

> ***ANSWER:*** *Divorce, the end result of failure to cleave, is one of the few things in the Bible which God specifically says He hates. He feels this way because He created us with a need for oneness that can only be met by the cleaving of marriage. He planned marriage to accomplish purposes which are of great value to Him (we discussed these in Session Two) and He wants us to experience what is best.*

**5.** What are some reasons why commitment is important to a marriage relationship? Why is your mate's commitment important to you?

> ***ANSWER:*** *Commitment is the only way to provide a person with the freedom to be real without fear of rejection.*

# C. PHASE 3—BECOME ONE FLESH (GENESIS 2:24C) *(10-15 minutes)*

**1.** The third step in the construction process is to "become one flesh"—to establish physical intimacy. What insights does Matthew 19:6 add to your understanding of becoming one flesh?

*ANSWER: The obvious meaning of becoming "one flesh" is for the husband and wife to establish physical intimacy with one another. The Hebrew term "flesh" clearly refers to the body, and the word "one" is from a root meaning "to unify." Matthew 19:6 makes it clear that God not only approves of sexual intimacy in marriage, but is the initiator of the process. No human influences should be allowed to interfere with such a union.*

*TIP: Read aloud the complete text of Genesis 2:24 before asking Question 1.*

*NOTE: You might find your group becomes a little quiet with these questions about sex. That's okay— it's to be expected.*

**2.** How is becoming one flesh something that happens at a point in time as well as an ongoing process?

*ANSWER: In one sense, physical intimacy is established each time a couple becomes one sexually. In another sense, the intimacy that is gained through sexual union carries over into all other areas of the relationship.*

**3.** Why is becoming one flesh important in achieving oneness in marriage?

> **ANSWER:** *Physical union is an expression of oneness with the total person, uniting spirit, soul and body.*

**4.** List the three most romantic times you and your mate have experienced:

> **TIP:** *Have each individual respond to this question privately for two or three minutes, then instruct participants to share their lists with their mates. Then have them work together to answer the next question among themselves before sharing with the group.*

Share the list with your mate. Then together, look for a common thread in these incidents which drew you together and which you can share with the group.

---

**HOMEBUILDERS PRINCIPLE #7:**

**A godly marriage is established and experienced as we leave, cleave and become one flesh.**

---

# D. THE RESULT—NAKED AND UNASHAMED (GENESIS 2:25) *(5 minutes)*

**1.** The result of Adam and Eve fulfilling the three phases of construction was that they were "naked and unashamed." What is the significance of a couple's being "naked and unashamed"? How is this a picture of oneness?

*ANSWER: This meant more than their physical nakedness. It also meant they were completely "transparent" with one another, feeling no threat in revealing themselves to their mate. What better picture of oneness could there be?*

**2.** Why is your acceptance of and commitment to your mate important in achieving openness and transparency in your relationship? What additional light does 1 John 4:18 shed on this process?

> There is no fear in love;
> but perfect love casts out fear.
> 1 John 4:18

*ANSWER: No one can be fully open with another as long as there is fear of how that person will react. Fear cannot be argued or wished away; only love, expressed in total acceptance and commitment, is strong enough to defeat it.*

*TIP: Point out that this question calls for a summary of all that has been discussed in this session, pushing each person to think personally about his or her marriage relationship. After a few moments for thought, invite volunteers to share their responses to the question.*

# Construction

(to be completed as a couple)
*(15-20 minutes)*

*Three separate* **Construction** *projects are provided to allow each couple to focus on the phase which they feel is most important for them to explore. Rather than trying to discuss issues in* *all three phases, it is best for a couple to examine just one area and agree on one action they will take in the coming week.*

*Instruct everyone to meet privately with their mate and together choose to complete one of the three **Construction** projects. Call attention to the last point at the end of the project ("LIST ONE ACTION...") which is to be completed regardless of the phase they decide to do. Explain that they will be asked to share with the group one insight from the phase they choose.*

Meet with your mate and choose one of these three projects:

## A. Phase 1—Leave (Work Together.)

**1.** In what ways have either you or your mate not left your parents?

**2.** What action(s) do you need to take while still honoring your parents?

## B. Phase 2—Cleave (Answer Individually, Then Share.)

**1.** What three things communicate cleaving/commitment:

to you?

to your mate?

**2.** What are some areas in which you are not cleaving?

## C. Phase 3—Become One Flesh (Write Answers Individually and Discuss on the Way Home.)

**1.** How can I improve our sex life?

**2.** What do you wish I would or wouldn't do in making love?

**3.** What do you enjoy most about our sex life?*

LIST ONE ACTION you will take this week to apply what you have learned:

*Call the group back together and ask each couple to share one insight from their **Construction** project.*

# ⌂Make a Date

Make a date with your mate to meet in the next few days to complete **HomeBuilders Project #4**. Your leader will ask at the next session for you to share one thing from this experience.

_____   _____   _____
Date                 Time                  Location

*The last three questions taken from *The Questions Book for Marriage Intimacy* by Dennis and Barbara Rainey. Published by FamilyLife, 1988.

# Recommended Reading

**The Questions Book for Marriage Intimacy**, by Dennis and Barbara Rainey.

This short book offers 31 questions you've probably never thought to ask your mate. These questions will ignite your curiosity and rekindle your fascination for each other. These questions will spark many memorable hours of sharing, sharpen your understanding of your mate and stimulate closeness in new areas of your marriage.

**Staying Close**, by Dennis Rainey.

Chapters 18-22 contain useful information that expands upon what we've covered in this session.

*Refer to the **Recommended Reading** and to **HomeBuilders Project #4**. Point out that three separate projects are provided, again allowing a couple to focus on one of the three phases of constructing a marriage. Suggest that if a couple feels they have unresolved issues remaining from their **Construction** project, they may prefer to tackle the same phase in their **HomeBuilders Project**. However, if they feel satisfied with their completion of the **Construction** project, it may be best to explore a different phase during the week.*

*Call attention to Session Five, "Fitting Together." Explain that the next session will focus on God's blueprint of specific responsibilities husbands and wives have in building oneness in their marriage. In order to deal in depth with each partner's role (and to allow each partner the freedom to respond without the mate doing any elbow-jabbing), the entire session will be conducted in separate groups for men and women. Also, this session will require 30 minutes more time than any of the others. Decide on the best starting and ending times to enable group members to make child-care arrangements.*

*Dismiss with a time of prayer, followed by refreshments and fellowship. Remember to be fair with your group by ending on time, even if some of the content cannot be fully covered.*

# HOMEBUILDERS PROJECT #4

## As a Couple: 5-10 minutes

Review the three phases of constructing a great marriage: leave, cleave and become one flesh. Then select one of the following projects that is most relevant to your marriage today.

## Individually: 25-30 minutes

PHASE 1 PROJECT—**LEAVING PARENTS**
PHASE 2 PROJECT—**CLEAVING**
PHASE 3 PROJECT—**BECOMING ONE FLESH**

### PHASE 1 PROJECT
### LEAVING PARENTS

**1.** Use the following chart to rank yourself and your mate in each area of leaving your parents:

| No Dependence on Parents | | Total Dependence on Parents |
|---|---|---|
| (<————————>) | | |
| 0  1  2  3  4  5 | | |
| Yourself | | Your Mate |
| 0  1  2  3  4  5 | Financial Dependence | 0  1  2  3  4  5 |
| 0  1  2  3  4  5 | Social Dependence | 0  1  2  3  4  5 |
| 0  1  2  3  4  5 | Emotional Dependence | 0  1  2  3  4  5 |
| 0  1  2  3  4  5 | Acceptance & Approval | 0  1  2  3  4  5 |
| 0  1  2  3  4  5 | Loyalty | 0  1  2  3  4  5 |

**2.** List any actions you may need to take.

**3.** List any suggestions you have for your mate and note how you can help him/her avoid dependence on parents.

Now turn to the end of the **HomeBuilders Project** and complete the section entitled "Interact as a Couple."

## PHASE 2 PROJECT
## CLEAVING

**1.** Answer the following Yes/No, True/False questions.

| | | |
|---|---|---|
| Y | N | Do you ever threaten to leave your mate? |
| T | F | My mate is secure in my commitment to him/her. |
| T | F | I am more committed to my mate than to my career. |
| T | F | My mate knows I am more committed to him/her than to my career. |
| T | F | I am more committed to my mate than to my activities. |
| Y | N | Do you emotionally leave your mate by withdrawing for an extended period of time because of conflict? |
| Y | N | Do you mentally leave your mate by staying preoccupied with other things? |
| Y | N | Are you passive about helping your mate solve his/her problems? |
| Y | N | Are you interested in your mate's needs and actively doing what you can to meet them? |

**2.** Now go back through the above list and determine in what areas you need to demonstrate a stronger commitment to your mate.

| Area | **COMMITMENT TO CLEAVE** Action Point |
|---|---|

**3.** Do you need to ask your mate's forgiveness in an area? If so, in which one(s)?

**4.** Write out your plan for communicating your commitment to your mate. Be specific.

## Phase 3 Project
## BECOMING ONE FLESH

### Becoming one flesh at a point in time.

**1.** How has leaving and cleaving made becoming one flesh easier? What changes do you need to make in these areas?

**2.** What circumstances or settings seem best for you to share intimately with one another? List a few.

**3.** What attitudes need to be present in you and your mate as you come together?

**4.** Write your mate a note: "It pleases me most when you..."

## Becoming one flesh over a lifetime.

**1.** How are you more one flesh now than when you first married?

**2.** In what one or two areas of your marriage do you need to continue to work at being one with one another?

**3.** Looking into the future, write a letter to your mate of what you expect your relationship to be like when you are both in your 70s or 80s. Include in this how you will feel about him/her, how you will have shared both good and bad and how you will have weathered storms together. Talk about how you envision your last 10 to 15 years together. Read your letter to him or her.

Now complete the section below.

## Interact as a Couple: 15-20 minutes

**1.** Share what both of you wrote in completing your project. Look each other in the eyes as you discuss your writings.

**2.** Work together to identify one or two actions for you to take in the coming week in response to your discussion.

**3.** Make a date as soon as possible to have a two- or three-hour block of time to be alone together for more communication.

Remember to bring your calendar for **Make a Date**
to the next session.

# FITTING TOGETHER– HUSBANDS

## OBJECTIVES

You will help the husbands learn to fit together with their wives as you guide them to:

- Identity the biblical responsibilities a husband has to his wife;
- Discuss hurdles that interfere with fulfilling these responsibilities;
- Choose specific actions to fulfill these responsibilities; and
- Commit to being accountable to the other husbands in fulfilling these responsibilities.

## OVERALL COMMENTS

1. In this session, you will split the group into two sections—husbands and wives. Both group leaders should read these two pages.
2. In this session you will tackle one of the most difficult and controversial topics today in the Christian church—roles for husbands and wives. Most couples do not clearly understand

what the Bible says about submission and headship, and will come in with preconceived ideas.

The irony is that, no matter how much people believe that there should be no roles in marriage, in reality there are no role-less relationships. Every married couple lives out roles in their relationship to one another, to their children and to others whom they contact.

It is important that you look through both the men's and women's sections to see what each group will be discussing. More than anything else, you'll need to challenge them to set aside their preconceived ideas and look at what the Bible says about these subjects—not at what they think, or what the culture thinks.

Also, realize that many of the arguments against men's and women's roles have their root in the way men and women have acted out those roles in the past. In the name of "being head of the home," for example, many men have ruled their homes almost as dictators. A true understanding of Scripture could open some eyes.

3. The session requires 30 more minutes than the other sessions. You'll need to alert all group members as to the starting and finishing times so they can make any necessary arrangements (e.g., baby-sitters).

Another option is to divide this session into two separate parts. Here are some pros and cons to help you decide what you wish to do:

PROS—You will be able to cover the material more in depth and at a relaxed pace. Spreading the study over two weeks allows time for group members to more fully consider the implications of these truths.

CONS—You will be extending the series one session longer, risking possible conflicts for continued attendance by all group members. Some people may not feel comfortable spending two sessions separated from their mate. Be sensitive to people who may be reluctant to be accountable to the group. Inform all participants, before they select actions to carry out, that they will be asked to be accountable to the group for at least one action they want to do. This sharing is a helpful means of gaining sympathetic support from others who are also working on improving their role in marriage.

4. Each group member is asked to become accountable to the group to report back next session on experiences in carrying out the actions planned during this session.

5. You'll need to arrange for a competent leader for the other group. Your mate is probably the logical one to fill this role, but if she is uncomfortable with leading, you may prefer to ask another group member to lead.

6. Finally, note that there are more **Construction** exercises than normal—three for the husbands and four for the wives.

# *Focus*

There are three biblical responsibilities God wants a husband to assume toward his wife: servant-leadership, unselfish loving, and caring.

# *Warm Up*
*(15-20 minutes)*

*This **Warm Up** is intended to help the husbands recognize a few challenges involved in being a husband and to admit—at least to themselves—that they need some help in meeting those challenges.*

*Before beginning the material in the study guide, why not consider asking the men in your group to open up and be honest with this group of men? Explain that there are very few times in life when men really have the opportunity to open up and admit where they need help as husbands. Share that you want this session to be more than just shallow talking, but as is appropriate, a sharing of what is really going on in your heart, life and role as a husband. That's how you can really come alongside and help one another.*

*Begin this session by asking each man to share one insight into marriage which he gained from completing* **Home-Builders Project #4**. *Ask for a show of hands of those who did the project. Do not chide those who did not, but encourage them to complete it and, if needed, make up unfinished projects. Have two people share (the purpose of this is for accountability). Congratulate those who did and underscore the importance of doing the project for each session.*

**1.** What various roles must you fill to be a success as a man in our society today?

> **ANSWER:** *Husband, father, provider, lover, employer/employee, etc. Success today is usually evaluated not in terms of our relationships, but of our status at work, size of our house and our accumulation of wealth.*

> **TIP:** *Ask the group for suggestions in answer to Question 1.*

**2.** What kinds of preparation (schooling, training courses, books, etc.) did you have for filling these roles?

> **ANSWER:** *Lead the group to see that some roles involve significant training requirements and opportunities, but being a husband is something people seem to expect can be done with little or no preparation. Many men didn't have an effective role model of a husband in their father. Ask the men to share what kind of model they had in their dad—good and bad.*

**3.** What factors in society and within marriage make it difficult today to be an effective husband? What is your greatest struggle in being a good husband?

> **POSSIBLE ANSWER:** *In society: We're under pressure to succeed in our careers, and sometimes to spend extra hours at work. After years of attacks in our culture about the roles of men and women, many men are unsure of how to relate to their wives. Our culture is so saturated with sexual images that it can be hard to remain true to your wife.*
>
> *Within marriage: Usually we're unprepared to deal with differences between men and women, and the different needs and desires both sexes bring into a relationship. Add this to the natural selfishness of human beings, and it's difficult to maintain a good relationship.*

> **TIP:** *Allow several minutes for discussion. If some men begin to vent frustrations about their wives or about women in general, explain that the focus of this session will not be on pointing out where our wives may be off base, but to discover ways men can become more successful as husbands.*

Oneness results when a couple follows God's blueprints, receives one another as God's gift, and then constructs their marriage by leaving parents, cleaving to each other and becoming one flesh. In this session, we will discover what character traits are essential if we are to be the husbands God created us to be.

It is vital that you understand from Scripture your responsibility as a husband. Only as you and your wife understand the unique roles which God has given to you can the oneness God intended in marriage be obtained.

> **TIP:** *Introduce the topic for this session: "In our culture, there are many voices telling men and women what they ought to be like. Because of the vast changes in women's roles that have*

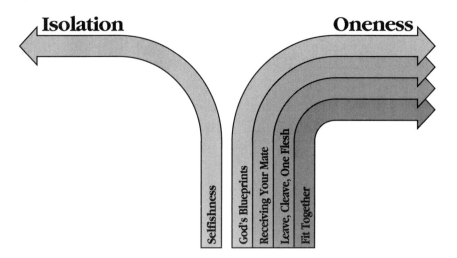

occurred during the past two decades, many men find it hard to relate to this 'new woman.' It will not be possible in this session to answer all the needs and questions which may be raised. Even though you may feel somewhat frustrated that some issue did not get explored as thoroughly as you wished, our goal is that you will come out of this with at least one or two actions to help you more successfully fit yourself with your wife in your role as husband."

Because there is a great deal of confusion about the roles of men and women today, this session will be spent helping you write a biblical job description for being a husband—the head of your home.

**TIP:** *As you begin this segment, read aloud the following paragraph: "The remainder of this session deals with 'core roles,' not comprehensive life-styles or specific tasks. These roles are never presented as describing the totality of a person's life, but as a central focus around which a person may build varied interests and involvements. All other forms of employment, recreation and ministry will naturally vary in intensity and importance* *in different stages of life. At no time, however, can husband or wife allow any other enterprise to infringe upon or usurp his or her core role. By stressing both mutual responsibility to the core roles and flexibility and creativity in building a life-style around them, you will help participants get over the emotional threat and misunderstanding that some will bring to this topic. It is crucial to avoid the common errors of either throwing out the biblical roles or forcing people to limit themselves totally within those roles. While people may have many questions and misgivings at this point, assure them that God's intent for their marriage is always for their benefit. The core roles are best because they are part of God's perfect design."*

## A. THE FIRST RESPONSIBILITY— BECOMING A SERVANT-LEADER
*(20-25 minutes)*

**1.** How is a husband's position as leader illustrated in Ephesians 5:23?

> **ANSWER:** *Husband leads the wife as Christ leads the church.*

> **TIP:** *Point out that the responsibility of husbands which is most frequently mentioned in the Bible is that of leadership in the home. However, there are many different ideas of what leadership involves. Many men have justified very selfish actions which are in complete opposition to the biblical goal of oneness, claiming the Bible supports their demands for privileges as "head of the house."*

> **OPTION:** *Ask group members to identify some typical images of leadership which are common in our society (the drill sergeant, the football coach, the corporation executive, the orchestra conductor, dictator, etc.). After*

*a variety of leadership roles have been mentioned, ask the men to suggest personal qualities that society associates with these leaders (strength, authority, power, dominance, decisiveness, superiority, knowledge, a person who never admits having needs, etc.). Point out that in order to build oneness in a marriage, a husband needs to be careful to take his model of leadership from Scripture, not from society.*

**2.** What are the responsibilities involved in being "the head" of your wife, a group of people, or an organization?

*ANSWER: Being aware of all factors in a situation. Being sensitive to the needs and desires of those involved. Helping those involved to succeed, making decisions. Accepting the consequences of the decisions.*

*TIP: Point out that leadership is much more of a responsibility than a privilege. Ask for several men to respond to Question 2. Accept the answers that are suggested, making sure that various facets of responsibility are mentioned. Ask the men to share where they may need to grow.*

**3.** What additional insights do you gain about leadership from Mark 10:42-45? What is servant-leadership?

*ANSWER: Jesus made a clear contrast between the "superior leader," who focuses on authority and status, and the "servant-leader," who focuses on giving of self to the ones he leads. The servant-leader does not lord authority over others, but willingly serves the needs of all. He does not demand service from others; rather, he gives up his own life and desires for others to have life—whether they deserve it or not.*

**4.** Which of those concepts is the most profound to you as you think of your leadership in your home? Why?

> **TIP:** *Instruct each man to write down a brief response to Question 4. After two or three minutes, read your answer, then ask each man to read what he wrote down.*

**5.** How would becoming a servant-leader change a man who:

a. tends to be **passive** and not accept his responsibilities?

> **ANSWER:** *This wouldn't mean attempting to transform his personality to become a "take charge" type of man, because God doesn't want him to become something he isn't. It would mean taking his responsibilities seriously and begin initiating opportunities to serve his wife and meet her needs. Also, many husbands like this tend to let their wives do much of the work around the house—cleaning, caring for children, etc. It would mean getting involved.*

b. is **dictatorial** and refuses to listen to his wife?

> **ANSWER:** *A dictatorial leader is the opposite of a servant-leader. A husband like this would need to begin looking for ways to serve instead of control. He would involve his wife in decisions, and would be concerned with her fulfillment. When there's a disagreement, it might even mean making a conscious choice to put aside his own desires and go by what his wife wants. It also would mean taking a strong look at how he can get involved with his wife in household responsibilities and child-rearing.*

**6.** How would becoming a servant-leader affect the ability of your wife to be submissive? How would she respond in other areas if you were more of a servant-leader?

*ANSWER: Many husbands complain that their wives are "not submissive" and fail to take a look at how they are doing in their own role as servant-leader.*

*A husband's servant-leadership is the only thing that makes a wife's submission reasonable. A passive husband makes submission impossible and a domineering husband makes submission intolerable. True submission is a response to a husband's true servant-leadership.*

*TIP: Point out that one of the roles the wives are examining is that of submission. Here is some of what they're learning:*

■ *That it's detrimental to take on the role of competitor with your husband. The husband is in need of help to fill the gaps in his life, compensating for his imbalances and blind spots. A helper brings assistance to those weaknesses so that the husband can succeed. A competitor does just the opposite, exploiting those weaknesses for her own advantage and superiority. A competitor also stirs a man to aggression and retaliation—or to withdrawal—rather than to caring and support to meet the woman's needs.*

■ *Submission does not require a wife to violate other scriptural commands or principles. The Bible does not ask wives to submit to sinful or damaging demands.*

---

### HOMEBUILDERS PRINCIPLE FOR MEN #1:

## A husband who is becoming a servant-leader is one who is in the process of denying himself daily for his wife.

---

### RESPONSIBILITY ONE:
## BECOMING A SERVANT-LEADER
*(10-15 minutes)*

List one to three practical ways in which you can demonstrate servant-leadership to your wife in the coming weeks:

*TIP: After allowing time to write their answers, ask each man to share one idea from his list. Suggest that any ideas that are shared are fair game for others to add to their lists if they so desire.*

*Explain that later in the session each man will be asked to choose one specific action and to be accountable to the group to carry it out before the next session.*

*OPTIONS: If you choose to divide this session into two sessions, rather than one extended meeting, end the first session by having each man choose one act of servant-leadership he will agree to carry out by the next session. Encourage the men to make a note of each group member's choice so that they can hold each other accountable at the next meeting.*

*You may want to pair the men off (especially if you have already been having couples maintaining contact with each other between the sessions) and have them check with each other before the next session to see how each is carrying out his plan.*

*Another idea: If time allows (and the wives' session is still going strong) lead the men in planning a surprise for the wives at the conclusion of this series. Consider a dinner out, a concert, play, picnic, party, etc.*

# Blueprints

## B. THE SECOND RESPONSIBILITY— UNSELFISH LOVING *(15 minutes)*

**1.** According to Ephesians 5:25-27, why is the second responsibility of a husband so important?

*ANSWER: Lead the group to recognize that leadership that is not motivated by love can lead to tyranny and servitude that is not motivated by love will lead to drudgery and resentment. In addition, the key to this type of love is that it is unselfish, not trying to possess the beloved, but to benefit her. Unselfish love is always demonstrated by giving of self, not just of things.*

*TIP: If the discussion on Question 1 begins to touch on the wife's reaction to unselfish love, call attention to the next question.*

**2.** How does this kind of love, this denial of self, communicate love to your wife? Why is this so important?

*ANSWER: Many wives have not seen their husbands deny themselves since courtship, and many others have never seen it at all. A husband's unselfish love frees the wife from her own selfishness, defeating isolation and building oneness.*

**3.** How does God describe love in these other passages?

Philippians 2:3

*ANSWER: Humble, regarding the one loved as being more important than self.*

1 Corinthians 13:4-7

*ANSWER: Patient, kind, not jealous, not bragging, not arrogant, not selfish, etc.*

John 15:13

*ANSWER: Gives up his own life and desires for the one loved.*

*TIP: Divide the group into pairs. Assign each pair to read one of the Scriptures listed under Question 3, looking for God's descriptions of love. If you have fewer than six men in the group, assign each man one passage to read and consider. After two or three minutes, ask each pair (or individual) to share what they discovered.*

**4.** Which of the preceding descriptions of love is the most profound to you? Why?

> **TIP:** *Share your own response in this time of personal expression.*

**5.** Which of those descriptions of love does your wife need most? How can you demonstrate that love to her?

---
### HOMEBUILDERS PRINCIPLE FOR MEN #2:

## The husband who is becoming an unselfish lover of his wife is one who is putting his wife's needs above his own.
---

# Construction

## RESPONSIBILITY TWO:
## UNSELFISH LOVING
*(5-10 minutes)*

*This section asks men to identify appropriate actions to apply the truth being studied.*

**1.** List five things you enjoy that could, if denied, demonstrate unselfish love to your wife.

> ***TIP:*** *Share with the men one of your own answers to Question 1. Invite volunteers to share a few other ideas, seeking to identify a variety of possible actions that might stimulate some new ideas for each man in the group.*
>
> *Instruct each man to choose one act from the list that would communicate love to his wife. Ask each man to tell what that action would be and why his wife would be likely to sense his love through it.*

**2.** What would you have to do in this self-denial to make it a willing act of love and not a grudging duty?

> ***TIP:*** *Point out (if it has not already been mentioned in the discussion) that any act of self-denial will only communicate love if it is perceived as being done willingly. Ask the men to suggest things they might need to do to ensure that they communicate willingness and not reluctance. (Focus on the value of the person, not on the act itself. A good question to ask is, "Why is she worth it?")*

# *Blueprints*

## C. THE THIRD RESPONSIBILITY— CARING *(10-15 minutes)*

**1.** What does Ephesians 5:28-30 add to your view of your responsibility to your wife? Why is this truth important?

> ***ANSWER:*** *Loving a wife is compared with concern for a man's own body, indicating the highest level of care growing out of very intimate knowledge. Demonstrating unselfish love and care for a wife is the best means by which a husband's own needs are met. Caring involves nourishing (fostering growth and maturity) and cherishing (esteeming someone as a priority). Again, the example of Jesus is the standard to imitate for those who belong to Him.*

> ***TIP:*** *Call for a volunteer to read aloud Ephesians 5:28-30, asking the group to think about what new insights these verses provide about a husband's responsibilities.*

> ***OPTION:*** *As each point is suggested, ask the group to identify a specific example of how that truth could be put into practice within a husband-wife relationship. For example:*

> ■ *A man who seeks to love his wife as his own body would seek to understand and then care for his wife's needs.*
> ■ *A man who cares for his wife's needs first will find her capable of meeting his needs in return.*

> ■ *A man can nourish his wife by encouraging her to pursue areas in which she wants to grow (by studying, taking classes, trying new ways of doing things, etc.).*
>
> ■ *A man can cherish his wife by scheduling time with her as a priority before other demands fill his calendar.*
>
> ■ *A man can learn to follow Christ's example of caring by regularly studying biblical accounts of Jesus' life and praying for God's help to apply Jesus' example to specific family situations.*

**2.** "Nourish" means to foster growth. What elements of nourishment does your wife need from you to help her grow?

**3.** The term "cherish" is from the Greek word meaning "to incubate or brood," and indicates esteeming someone as a priority. How can you show your wife you esteem and value her? Be specific.

> *TIP: Divide the group in half and assign part of the men to discuss Question 2 while the rest of the group discusses Question 3. Allow several minutes for interaction, then invite one person from each group to report on the ideas they thought of for nourishing and cherishing their wives. Suggest that, as the men listen to these reports, they write down ideas that seem to fit their own wives.*
>
> *Comment that just as the wife's submission enables the husband to fulfill his role as servant-leader, so the husband's honor and praise enable the wife to fulfill her calling. The core roles can only be adequately fulfilled when the mate responds properly.*

*While we often hear exhortations for wives to submit, we rarely hear about the masculine counter-part to submission—honor and praise. Any man who is serious about his wife's fulfilling her role will make honor and praise priority ingredients in his response to her efforts. Without these she will feel that her role and tasks are inferior and secondary and will do what so many women in our society have done—go looking for something else that will make her feel good about herself.*

---

### HOMEBUILDERS PRINCIPLE FOR MEN #3:

## The husband who is becoming a caring head of his house is one who encourages his wife to grow and become all that God intended her to be.

---

# Construction

## RESPONSIBILITY THREE: CARING
*(15-20 minutes)*

**1.** One aspect of leadership is bringing appropriate resources to a situation to help others become successful. What resources do you need to use in order to nourish and cherish your wife so she can succeed as a woman, wife and mother (help with her schedule, assist with a problem, give or get direct help with a task, provide encouragement, spend time with her, etc.)?

*TIP: Read aloud the statement and Question 1. Point out the ideas suggested in the study guide, then share one way in which you need to help your wife succeed as a woman, wife and mother.*

*Then instruct each man to write down two or three specific ideas of his own, either personalizing one of those suggested or adding a new one. After several minutes, invite volunteers to share at least one idea they wrote down.*

**2.** Review the three **Construction** projects you have done in this session and choose one act of servant-leadership, unselfish loving, or caring for your wife which you will share with the group and for which you will agree to be accountable to the group by the next session.

*OPTION: You may want to pair the men off (especially if you have already been having couples maintain contact with each other between the sessions) and have them check with each other before the next session to see how each is doing in carrying out his plan. Guide the group in dividing into pairs. If the number of men is unequal, join with one person yourself. Instruct them to pray together concerning their efforts to fulfill their responsibilities as husbands.*

## Make a Date

Make a date with your mate to meet in the next few days to complete **HomeBuilders Project #5**. Your leader will ask at the next session for you to share one thing from this experience.

_____  _____  _____
Date                    Time                    Location

*Point out that there are separate projects for husbands and wives, both of which focus on identifying and meeting each other's needs. While the projects are to be done separately, suggest that they do them at the same time so that at an agreed-upon time they can check with each other to see if they have accurately listed each other's needs.*

## Recommended Reading

**Rocking the Roles**, by Robert Lewis and William Hendricks.

This book provides a balanced, biblical guide to understanding marital roles.

**Building Your Mate's Self-Esteem**, by Dennis and Barbara Rainey.

In this book you will find clues to understanding your wife's self-esteem, laws that will help you to free your mate from her past and building blocks to strengthen her self-esteem.

**The Questions Book for Marriage Intimacy**, by Dennis and Barbara Rainey.

This short book offers 31 questions you've probably never thought to ask your mate. These questions will ignite your curiosity and rekindle your fascination for each other. These questions will spark many memorable hours of sharing, sharpen your understanding of your mate and stimulate closeness in new areas of your marriage.

**Staying Close**, by Dennis Rainey.

Chapter 14—"The Making of a Servant-leader"—elaborates on the material covered in this session.

*Conclude the session with prayer. If you have completed this session in one meeting, it may be too late for people to remain for refreshments and fellowship. Be considerate of people's schedules in making your decision.*

# HOMEBUILDERS PROJECT #5—HUSBANDS

Set aside an hour and a half to complete this project.

**1.** Review the lesson on the responsibilities of a husband. (Complete any undone **Construction** projects.)

**2.** Ask God to show you how you are to be the best possible husband for your wife.

**3.** Make a list of 10 to 15 of your wife's needs, grouping them in the following areas of life (you may wish to schedule a special time to ask her what they really are):

| Physical | Social | Spiritual | Mental | Emotional |
|----------|--------|-----------|--------|-----------|
|          |        |           |        |           |
|          |        |           |        |           |
|          |        |           |        |           |
|          |        |           |        |           |

**4.** List three of the above needs which seem to be of greatest importance to her at this time.

**5.** After verifying these needs with your wife, list appropriate actions you need to take to help meet those needs, demonstrating your desire to be God's man in her life.

**6.** Pray again, asking God to give you wisdom and skill in meeting your wife's needs effectively.

**7.** Write your wife's needs on a 3×5-inch card and place it where you will see it daily (mirror, desk drawer, etc.) as a reminder of how you can meet her needs in a practical way.

**8.** Be prepared to share next time your successes and/or failures. Your responses will encourage others in the group.

Remember to bring your calendar for **Make a Date**
to the next session.

# FITTING TOGETHER— WIVES

## OBJECTIVES

You will help the wives learn to fit together with their husbands as you guide them to:

- Identify four biblical responsibilities a wife has to her husband;
- Discuss hurdles that interfere with fulfilling these responsibilities;
- Choose specific actions to fulfill these responsibilities; and
- Commit to being accountable to the other wives in fulfilling these responsibilities.

## OVERALL COMMENTS

1. In this session, you will split the group into two sections— husbands and wives. Both group leaders should read these two pages.
2. In this session you will tackle one of the most difficult and controversial topics today in the Christian church—roles for husbands and wives. Most couples do not clearly understand

what the Bible says about submission and headship, and will come in with preconceived ideas.

The irony is that, no matter how much people believe that there should be no roles in marriage, in reality there are no role-less relationships. Every married couple lives out roles in their relationship to one another, to their children and to others whom they contact.

It is important that you look through both the men's and women's sections to see what each group will be discussing. More than anything else, you'll need to challenge them to set aside their preconceived ideas and look at what the Bible says about these subjects—not at what they think, or what the culture thinks.

Also, realize that many of the arguments against men's and women's roles have their root in the way men and women have acted out those roles in the past. In the name of "being head of the home," for example, many men have ruled their homes almost as dictators. A true understanding of Scripture could open some eyes.

3. The session requires 30 more minutes than the other sessions. You'll need to alert all group members as to the starting and finishing times so they can make any necessary arrangements (e.g., baby-sitters).

Another option is to divide this session into two separate parts. Here are some pros and cons to help you decide what you wish to do:

PROS—You will be able to cover the material more in depth and at a relaxed pace. Spreading the study over two weeks allows time for group members to more fully consider the implications of these truths.

CONS—You will be extending the series one session longer, risking possible conflicts for continued attendance by all group members. Some people may not feel comfortable spending two sessions separated from their mate. Be sensitive to people who may be reluctant to be accountable to the group. Inform all participants, before they select actions to carry out, that they will be asked to be accountable to the group for at least one action they want to do. This sharing is a helpful means of gaining sympathetic support from others who are also working on improving their role in marriage.

4. Each group member is asked to become accountable to the group to report back next session on experiences in carrying out the actions planned during this session.
5. You'll need to arrange for a competent leader for the other group. Your mate is probably the logical one to fill this role, but if he is uncomfortable with leading, you may prefer to ask another group member to lead.
6. Finally, note that there are more **Construction** exercises than normal—three for the husbands and four for the wives.
7. Be aware that as these women come together, each one has different needs. One may just need to talk about the pressures she faces and listen to others do the same. Another woman may be angry and bitter about what the Bible says and find herself rebelling against what Scripture says she should do. Another may be discouraged because her husband gives no leadership and has the wrong priorities, making it extremely difficult for her to be supportive. And others will be very teachable, eager to learn and grow.

If a woman expresses anger or bitterness, it is best to thank her for being open with the group, then ask her to hold off making any final judgments until she has had an opportunity to consider the complete teaching of this session. Unless she raises issues which others in the group indicate are significant for them as well, it is better to meet with her privately after the session than to take more of the group's time to deal with her individual concerns.

There are four biblical responsibilities God wants a wife to assume toward her husband: making marriage a priority, unselfish love, submission, and respect.

# Warm Up
### (10-15 minutes)

*This **Warm Up** is intended to help the wives recognize a few challenges involved in being a wife and admit—at least to themselves, if not to the group—that they need some help in meeting those challenges.*

*Begin this session by asking the women to share one insight into marriage which each has gained from completing **Home-Builders Project #4**. Have two people share (the purpose of this is for accountability). Congratulate those who did the project and underscore the importance of doing the project for each session.*

**1.** List some words that describe each point of view:

|        | SOCIETY'S VIEW | GOD'S VIEW |
|--------|----------------|------------|
| Woman  |                |            |
| Wife   |                |            |
| Mother |                |            |

> **TIP:** *This second column of the chart will probably be harder to complete, illustrating the need to examine what Scripture indicates is God's view of a wife.*

**2.** Woman are being told today that they need to be successful. What do you think makes a successful wife?

> **TIP:** *After everyone has commented, follow up with this question, "What impact do you think the changing roles of men and women have had on wives, hus-*

*bands and marriage?" Allow several minutes for discussion.*

**3.** What are some of your struggles in trying to succeed as a wife?

> **TIP:** *Recognize that some of the answers to Question 2 may have gotten into this question as well, but it is helpful to admit to one another those areas where we personally find difficulties. Share one or two of your own responses to this question, then listen for indications of women experiencing confusion, pressure, or even bitterness about their circumstances. Some may want to vent their frustrations with what they see as their husband's inadequate leadership. Explain that the focus of this session will not be on pointing out where our husbands are off base, but to discover specific ways to become successful as a wife.*

Oneness results when a couple follows God's blueprints, receives one another as God's gift, and then constructs their marriage by leaving parents, cleaving to each other and becoming one flesh.

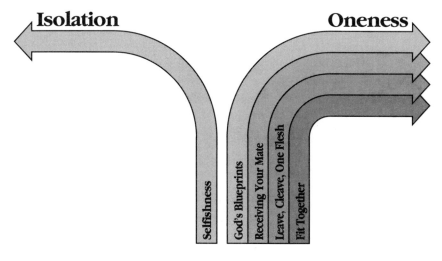

It is vital that you understand from Scripture your responsibility as a wife. Only as you and your husband understand the unique roles which God has given to you can the oneness God intended in marriage be obtained.

*TIP:* *Summarize your opening discussion and introduce the topic for this session: "In our culture, there are many voices telling men and women what they ought to be like. Because of the vast changes in women's roles that have occurred during the past few decades, many women find it difficult to relate to their role as a 'new woman.' It will not be possible in this one session to answer all the needs and questions that may be raised. So, even though it is likely you may feel frustrated that some issue was not explored as thoroughly as you wished, our goal is that you will come out of this with at least one or two actions to help you more deeply value your home and to help you successfully fit yourself with your husband."*

*TIP:* *As you begin this segment, read aloud the following paragraph: "The remainder of this session deals with 'core roles,' not comprehensive life-styles or specific tasks. These roles are never presented as describing the totality of a person's life, but as a central focus around which a person may build varied interests and involvements. All other forms of employment, recreation and ministry will naturally vary in intensity and importance in different stages of life. At no time, however, can husband or wife allow any other enterprise to infringe upon or usurp his or her core role. By stressing both mutual responsibility to the core roles and flexibility and creativity in building a life-style around them, you will help participants get over the emotional threat and misunderstanding that some will bring to this topic. It is crucial to avoid the common errors of either throwing out the biblical roles or forcing people to limit themselves totally within those roles. While people may have many questions and misgivings at this point, assure them that God's*

*intent for their marriage is always for their benefit. The core roles are best because they are part of God's perfect design."*

## A. THE FIRST RESPONSIBILITY— MAKING YOUR MARRIAGE A PRIORITY *(15-20 minutes)*

**1.** What does it mean for a wife to look "well to the ways of her household" (Proverbs 31:27)?

> ***ANSWER:*** *"Look well" conveys the idea that a wife is alert to the needs of her home. That, in turn, means that she makes it a priority.*
>
> ***TIP:*** *Explain that the last 21 verses of Proverbs describe "an excellent wife." Read aloud Proverbs 31:27, then ask volunteers to tell the meaning of to look "well to the ways of her household."*

**2.** What happens to your relationship with your husband when you do or do not "look well" to your marriage?

| WHEN I DO "LOOK WELL" | WHEN I DO NOT "LOOK WELL" |
|---|---|
|  |  |

> ***TIP:*** *Encourage those who do work outside the home to identify ways they find helpful to deal with schedule problems in order to make marriage their priority.*

**3.** In the "IDEAL WIFE" column below, rank these items by numbering them from 1-13 to show the priorities that make a successful wife. Then, in the "ME" column, show where your priorities currently are.

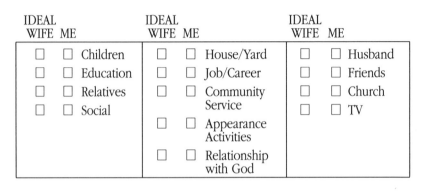

| IDEAL WIFE | ME | | IDEAL WIFE | ME | | IDEAL WIFE | ME | |
|---|---|---|---|---|---|---|---|---|
| ☐ | ☐ | Children | ☐ | ☐ | House/Yard | ☐ | ☐ | Husband |
| ☐ | ☐ | Education | ☐ | ☐ | Job/Career | ☐ | ☐ | Friends |
| ☐ | ☐ | Relatives | ☐ | ☐ | Community Service | ☐ | ☐ | Church |
| ☐ | ☐ | Social | ☐ | ☐ | Appearance Activities | ☐ | ☐ | TV |
| | | | ☐ | ☐ | Relationship with God | | | |

*TIP: Expect some differences in the relative ranking of the various items, but point out that the major tenet of this series is that "Relationship with God" and "Husband" need to be #1, and #2 in order for a wife to be building a marriage according to God's blueprints. Point out that very good things, (church, kids, community service, etc.) can drain what she has to offer her marriage.*

*Ask each person to go through the list of items again, this time marking in the "ME" column the order of importance she actually gave each item during the last week. After two or three minutes, divide the group into pairs. If there is an uneven number in the group, work as a partner with one person. Instruct each woman to share with her partner two items which most closely matched her ranking for the "Ideal Wife" and two items which were furthest out of line with the ideal. Allow several minutes for discussion.*

*Invite volunteers to tell what discussing this chart has said to them about where their main priority should be and how they feel they are doing in that area.*

**4.** How is the priority you place on your marriage reflected in your schedule?

> **TIP:** *Call on one or two different women to share how making marriage a priority would be reflected in her schedule. Be prepared to share any insights from your experience in scheduling your time to develop your relationship with your husband.*
>
> **OPTION:** *After people have responded, ask each one to tell one word or phrase she would like to have be a true description of her schedule, indicating how her use of time is a statement of her values.*

**5.** What advice would you give to:

a. the woman who is struggling with her priorities and works outside the home?

b. the woman who, though not struggling, has her priorities out of line?

---

**HOMEBUILDERS PRINCIPLE FOR WOMEN #1:**

**Becoming a successful wife requires that a woman make her husband her #2 priority after her relationship with God.**

---

**TIP:** *Call attention to **HomeBuilders Principle for Women #1** as a summary of this discussion.*

# Construction

## RESPONSIBILITY ONE:
## MAKING YOUR MARRIAGE A PRIORITY
### *(10-15 minutes)*

**1.** In what ways have you made your relationship with your husband a priority?

**2.** In what ways does your husband respond when he sees you making your marriage a priority?

> ***TIP:*** *Share one or two of your own ideas to help women think of possible things to write. After two or three minutes, invite volunteers to share one action which they wrote down and their husband's response. Hearing each other's stories may stimulate ideas they would not have thought of on their own.*

**3.** What are the biggest obstacles you face in making your marriage a priority?

**4.** What are three things that you can do to make your relationship with your husband your priority in the coming week? Be specific, practical and make it personal.

> *TIP: After several minutes, divide the group into pairs and have each woman share one answer she wrote, telling why she feels it is significant in her relationship with her husband.*

## Blueprints

## B. THE SECOND RESPONSIBILITY— UNSELFISH LOVE *(5-10 minutes)*

**1.** The apostle Paul wrote that older women should "encourage the younger women to love their husbands,..." (Titus 2:4). Why do you think this instruction is significant?

> *TIP: Instruct each woman to read Titus 2:4, and to think of reasons why the commands here ("to love their husbands, to love their children") are significant. Then invite ideas of how women can focus their affection on their family while balancing responsibilities outside the home.*

**2.** A problem in our society is that "love" is usually equated with a feeling. We need to look at Scripture to find the full definition of what love is. Write down the insights you gain about love from the following Scriptures:

1 Corinthians 13:4-7

> **ANSWER:** *Patient, kind, not jealous, not bragging, not arrogant, not selfish, etc.*

John 15:13

> **ANSWER:** *Giving up her own life and desires for the one loved.*

Philippians 2:3-4

> **ANSWER:** *Humble, regarding the one loved as being more important than self.*

> **TIP:** *Assign each pair of women one of the passages, looking for definitions of love. (If you have fewer than six women in the group, assign each person one passage to read and consider.) After two or three minutes, ask each pair (or individual) to share what they discovered.*

**3.** Which of these descriptions of love is the most profound to you in thinking about your relationship with your husband? Why?

> **TIP:** *Share your own response in this time of personal expression. You might wish to ask the group how they would apply their insight to their own situation.*

**4.** "The heart of her husband trusts in her" (Proverbs 31:11). Every wife wants a husband who is open, who will share his innermost person with her. Few women, however, realize how insecure and fearful their husbands really are. Your love for your husband has a profound impact on his trust of you and his willingness to be vulnerable.

Evaluate your husband's openness and trust towards you. How is your love affecting his willingness and ability to be transparent with you?

*TIP: Remind the group of "the excellent wife" in Proverbs 31. Read aloud the first half of verse 11 and the statement about the connection between a wife's love for her husband and his trust in her. Comment that biblical love always means seeking the highest good for the person loved; it focuses on actions, not emotions. A wife who commits to doing what is the highest good for her husband will earn her husband's trust.*

*Summarize this sharing by pointing out that oneness and distrust are in opposition to each other. Oneness involves total unity of body, emotions and will. Distrust will shatter oneness.*

---

## HOMEBUILDERS PRINCIPLE
### FOR WOMEN #2:

**The wife who is becoming an unselfish lover of her husband is one who is putting her husband's needs above her own.**

---

# Construction

## RESPONSIBILITY TWO:
## UNSELFISH LOVE
### (5 minutes)

**1.** In order to unselfishly love your husband and open your relationship, what rights to which you are clinging do you need to let go?

**2.** What three things communicate love to your husband? (Not what **you** think communicates love, but what **he** thinks.)

**3.** What practical way can you demonstrate unselfish love to your husband this week?

**TIP:** *After several minutes, ask each woman to tell one answer she wrote. Share an answer of your own as part of this time of personal expression.*

**OPTION:** *If you choose to divide this lesson into two sessions rather than one extended meeting, end the first session by having the women each choose one action to make marriage a priority or to demonstrate unselfish love that they will agree to carry out in the coming week. Encourage the wives to make a note of each group member's choice so that they can hold each other accountable at the next meeting.*

*You may want to pair the women off (especially if you have already been having couples maintain contact with each other between the sessions) and have them check with each other to see how each is doing in carrying out her plan before the next session.*

## *Blueprints*

## C. THE THIRD RESPONSIBILITY— SUBMISSION *(15-20 minutes)*

*TIP: Sometime during this section you may find it helpful to briefly tell the women some of what their husbands are learning about the concept of "headship." For example, they're learning about the concept of being a "servant-leader" as opposed to a "dictatorial leader." Most arguments against roles in marriage stem from the fact that many men throughout history have been dictatorial leaders of their homes. Servant-leadership, however, may be a new concept to many.*

**1.** According to Ephesians 5:22, a wife should demonstrate both an attitude of submission and the actions that result from it. What reactions does the idea of submission generate among women? Why?

*ANSWER: The very word, "submission" causes a negative reaction in many women today. It conjures up images of a husband ordering his wife around and forcing her to do his will, and the wife meekly responding to his every wish.*

**2.** Why is submission seen as a threat to women?

*ANSWER: Because they feel it demeans their status and puts them in a role of inferiority.*

*TIP: Some of the answers to Question 1 may also apply to Question 2. After a few minutes of discussion, point out that the biblical view of submission is very different from the common ideas of inferiority, loss of identity, or blind obedience that many people assume. Be sure the women notice that the attitude the wife should have toward her husband ("be subject to") is qualified by the phrase, "as to the Lord." This conveys the sense of transferring to the husband the same love and trust given to God.*

**3.** In what areas do you struggle with submission?

*TIP: Share one care of your relationship with your husband in which you struggle with submission. Then ask each woman to tell of one area of similar struggle in her marriage. As different women speak, the others should be thinking of whether each area shared is one that affects her as well.*

**4.** What does Scripture say is involved in submission?

1 Peter 2:21-23

*ANSWER: Jesus set the example for submission by enduring injustice, trusting Himself to God's care.*

1 Peter 3:1,2

*ANSWER: Submission demonstrates purity and respect and can influence a husband for good.*

1 Peter 3:3,4

**ANSWER:** *Submission reflects gentleness and is prized by God.*

1 Peter 3:5,6

**ANSWER:** *The wife who submits does not need to fear, for she is doing right.*

Titus 2:5

**ANSWER:** *Submission is part of being sensible, pure and kind—and brings honor to God's Word.*

**TIP:** *Assign each woman one of the Scripture references in the study guide to read and report on words or phrases that describe something about what submission involves. If you have fewer than five women in the group, share the information in the verses not assigned. Allow a minute or two for reading and thinking before calling on women to share what they discovered.*

**COMMENT:** *"Submission comes from two Greek words meaning 'under' and 'arrange or complete.' The sense of the term is to voluntarily organize or fit into or under in a way that makes a complete whole."*

**OPTION:** *Read aloud 1 John 4:18, then ask what submission has to do with the truth that "perfect love casts out fear." (A person who truly loves and is loved by someone will not be afraid to submit—voluntarily fit—to that person.)*

**5.** Why is submission to your husband important:

a. to his leadership?

> ***ANSWER:*** *Willing submission makes it possible for a man to exercise servant-leadership. Assertion or unwillingness forces a man to either become passive, become a manipulator, or become dictatorial.*

b. to his love for you?

> ***ANSWER:*** *Willing submission makes it easy for a man to exercise unselfish love. Unwillingness tends to encourage response in kind, resulting in isolation and loss of oneness.*

c. to his care for you?

> ***ANSWER:*** *Submission makes a man more aware of his responsibility to nourish and cherish.*

d. to his trust of you?

> ***ANSWER:*** *Trust grows in a climate free of competition and selfish desire.*
>
> ***TIP:*** *Ask a different woman to respond to each of the parts of Question 5.*

**6.** What advice would you give to help a wife submit to a husband:

a. who is **passive** and doesn't lead?

b. who is a **dictator**, doesn't listen and demands submission?

> **TIP:** *Ask for volunteers to suggest advice to help a wife submit to a husband—expect group members to raise some deeply felt concerns. The focus of this discussion should not be trying to identify specific actions that "solve" every situation, but rather to engage group members in a few minutes of envisioning obedient actions and attitudes in difficult situations.*
>
> *Point out that this is where most wives encounter their biggest problem in submitting. The natural inclination is to say, "I'll submit when he does his part correctly." While fitting together with someone who pleases us is very agreeable, it is precisely those times when disagreements arise that it is most necessary to respond "as to the Lord," trusting His perfect wisdom and following His example. When a wife allows herself to get into a power struggle with her husband, she risks costing both of them the oneness necessary for their relationship to grow.*
>
> *CAUTION: Submission does not require a wife to violate other scriptural commands or principles. The Bible does not ask wives to submit to sinful or damaging demands. If the issue of spouse abuse is raised, remind them of these passages that provide wise counsel:*
>
> > ■ *Proverbs 14:7 says to "leave the presence of a fool." This does not mean divorce; it simply*

*advises making enough space to avoid the influence of the fool.*

■ *Romans 5:8 shares Christ's example of loving the sinner even though hating sin (Psalm 45:7). An abusive husband needs help, not silence.*

■ *Romans 13:1 and 1 Peter 2:13-15 teach God's establishment of governmental authority to control those who do wrong. A wife in danger should not hesitate to contact the authorities for protection.*

*Summarize this discussion by reading aloud.*

---

**HOMEBUILDERS PRINCIPLE FOR WOMEN #3:**

### In order for a husband to successfully lead, he must have a wife who willingly submits to his leadership.

---

*Construction*

## RESPONSIBILITY THREE: SUBMISSION

*(5-10 minutes)*

What are two ways (two areas) that you can demonstrate submission to your husband? (Be sure to select areas that would really encourage him, not just the areas that would be easiest for you.)

**TIP:** *Share one or two examples of ways you demonstrate sub-*

*mission to your husband. Instruct each woman to privately write two ways that she can demonstrate submission to her husband. After a few moments, ask each woman to join with another member of the group and share one idea of how to foster submission with their husbands.*

## *Blueprints*

## D. THE FOURTH RESPONSIBILITY— RESPECT *(10 minutes)*

And let the wife see that she respects and reverences her husband—that she notices him, regards him, honors him, prefers him, venerates and esteems him; and that she defers to him, praises him, and loves and admires him exceedingly (Ephesians 5:33b, *AMP*).

**1.** What are three observations from this paragraph of what it means to respect your husband?

*TIP: Work in pairs to write three observations about what this paragraph says it means for a wife to respect her husband. After a few minutes, ask each pair to share their observations.*

**2.** Why do men need their wives' respect? Why is respect important to an insecure man? What are some specific reasons that **your** husband needs **your** respect?

*ANSWER:* Respect builds a man's confidence, his trust and his desire to live up to this admiration.

*OPTION:* Ask one or two follow-up questions to emphasize the practical implications of respect: "What happens to a man who is not respected by his wife? How can a wife show respect to her husband if she does not really admire him?" (Focus on his strengths, his attributes which are appealing to her, areas in which they are in agreement, the value of their relationship, etc.)

Then ask each woman to identify at least one specific way her husband needs her respect. Share one or two examples of your own if needed to stimulate ideas.

**3.** How do you communicate your respect to your husband?

---

**HOMEBUILDERS PRINCIPLE
FOR WOMEN #4:**

### A successful wife is one who respects her husband.

---

## *Construction*

## **RESPONSIBILITY FOUR: RESPECT**
*(15 minutes)*

**1.** Thoughtfully list some additional ways that you can verbally and actively show respect to your husband. (Think back to those times when he has exemplified confidence in his ability as a man.)

| VERBALLY | ACTIVELY |
|---|---|
| 1. | 1. |
| 2. | 2. |
| 3. | 3. |

> ***TIP:*** *After a few minutes, ask each person to share one idea from either list.*

**2.** Review the four **Construction** projects you have done in this session and choose **one** thing for which you will be accountable to the group to do before the next session—to make your marriage a priority, to express unselfish love, to willingly submit, or to show respect to your husband.

> ***TIP:*** *Guide the group in using the remaining time in the session to: share the action they wrote on their page; agree to be accountable to one another; and pray together concerning their efforts to fulfill their responsibilities as wives.*

Make a date with your mate to meet in the next few days to complete **HomeBuilders Project #5**. Your leader will ask at the next session for you to share one thing from this experience.

| Date | Time | Location |
|------|------|----------|

*Rejoin the husbands for a few moments to have the couples make a date to complete **HomeBuilders Project #5** this week.*

*There are separate projects for husbands and wives, both of which focus on identifying and meeting each other's needs. Couples should do their projects at the same time so that they can check with each other to see if they have accurately listed each other's needs.*

## Recommended Reading

**Rocking the Roles,** by Robert Lewis and William Hendricks.

This book provides a balanced, biblical guide to understanding marital roles.

**Building Your Mate's Self-Esteem,** by Dennis and Barbara Rainey.

In this book you will find clues to understanding your husband's self-esteem, laws that will help you to free your mate from his past and building blocks to strengthen his self-esteem.

**The Questions Book for Marriage Intimacy,** by Dennis and Barbara Rainey.

This short book offers 31 questions you've probably never thought to ask your mate. These questions will ignite your curiosity and rekindle your fascination for each other. These questions will spark many memorable hours of sharing, sharpen your understanding of your mate and stimulate closeness in new areas of your marriage.

**Staying Close**, by Dennis Rainey.
Chapter 15—"How to Love Your Husband" expands on the material discussed in this session.

*Conclude the session with prayer. If you have completed this session in one meeting, it may be too late for people to remain for refreshments and fellowship. Be considerate of people's schedules in making your decision.*

# HOMEBUILDERS PROJECT #5—WIVES
Set aside 60-90 minutes to complete the following project:

**1.** Review the lesson on the responsibilities of a wife. (Complete any undone **Construction** projects.)

**2.** Ask God to show you how you are to be the best possible wife for your husband.

**3.** Make a list of 10 to 15 of your husband's needs, grouping them in the following areas of life (you may wish to schedule a special time to ask him what they really are):

| Physical | Social | Spiritual | Mental | Emotional |
|----------|--------|-----------|--------|-----------|
|          |        |           |        |           |
|          |        |           |        |           |
|          |        |           |        |           |
|          |        |           |        |           |

**4.** List three of the above needs which seem to be of greatest importance to him at this time.

**5.** After verifying these needs with your husband, list appropriate actions you need to take to help meet those needs, demonstrating your desire to be God's woman in his life.

**6.** Pray again, asking God to give you wisdom and skill in meeting your husband's needs effectively.

**7.** Write your intended actions on a 3×5-inch card and place it where you will see it daily (mirror, purse, etc.) as a reminder of how you can meet his needs in practical ways.

**8.** Be prepared to share in the next session your successes as well as failures, so that you might encourage others in the group.

Remember to bring your calendar for **Make a Date** to the next session.

# BUILDING IN THE SPIRIT

## OBJECTIVES

You will help your group members learn to yield to the Spirit as individuals and as couples as you guide them to:

- Contrast a marriage without God and a marriage with God;
- Identify three key elements necessary for walking with the Holy Spirit;
- Discuss ways an individual and a couple can restore and maintain a relationship with the Spirit; and
- Pray by faith to confess known sin and to ask for the Spirit's filling.

## OVERALL COMMENTS

1. Before teaching this session, it will be helpful if you are familiar with these important booklets by Bill Bright (found in **Recommended Reading** for Session Six):

   *How to Be Sure You Are a Christian*
   *How to Experience God's Love and Forgiveness*
   *How to Be Filled with the Spirit*
   *How to Walk in the Spirit*

2. Consider arranging for a group member—or your mate—to share briefly about the Holy Spirit's ministry in his or her life and marriage. Meet with this person ahead of time to review

what will be shared, making sure it will be brief, practical and supportive of the concepts in the above booklets.

3. If anyone in your group has not yet received Christ as Savior, arrange to share Christ individually with him or her before this session.

4. Be prepared to begin the session with the husbands and wives in separate rooms for sharing their experiences in carrying out the actions planned at the previous session. Because this session contains several concepts to be taught, it will be important to keep your split group's time to 10 minutes. This session needs a full 60-90 minutes to be taught properly.

5. Before the next session, plan for you and your spouse to call each group member and inquire about any questions they have about this session. Ask, "Is there a specific area related to the Holy Spirit that I could be praying about with you?" Show your concern and be sensitive to people's spiritual struggles.

# *Focus*

A husband and wife can experience
true oneness only as they live by faith,
in the power of the Holy Spirit.

# *Warm Up*

*(15-20 minutes)*

*This **Warm Up** moves quickly from reviewing experiences resulting from the previous session to introducing the current topic. By this point in the series your group should have reached a healthy level of openness, but some may still need your support and encouragement.*

*OPTION: Begin this session with the husbands and wives in separate rooms for 8 to 10 minutes of sharing how things went in carrying out the actions planned during the previous session.*

*Encourage group members to ask each other questions such as:*

*Which of your plans do you feel went well?*
*What did you find was difficult?*
*How did your mate respond when you...?*
*What do you think you might do differently this next week?*
*What do you feel you want to keep on doing?*

**1.** Think back to the childhood tale of "The Three Little Pigs." What is the moral of the story?

*ANSWER: Diligence and hard work will win out against life's problems.*

**2.** Compare the lesson of "The Three Little Pigs" with the key point in Jesus' story of the wise and foolish builders (Matthew 7:24-27). What is similar in the two stories? What is the key difference in the conclusion of each story?

*ANSWER: The first two pigs and the fool did not build wisely, and their houses collapsed when trouble came. The third pig and the wise man did build wisely, and their houses weathered the trouble that came.*

*TIP: If your group seems unable to go beyond the obvious differences of pigs and a wolf in one story and men and a storm in the other, ask a follow-up question: "Do both the third pig and the wise man appear to have built successfully?" (Yes.) "What is the difference between the stories as to the key to such success?" (The story of the pigs infers that human effort and thought is adequate to overcoming trou-*

*ble. Jesus' story defines God's Word as the source of wisdom necessary to triumph over adversity and thus succeed.)*

**3.** What is the application for your marriage?

**ANSWER:** *According to the "Three Little Pigs," a husband and wife can build a solid home through careful planning and diligent effort. But according to Jesus' story, hearing and obeying God's Word is essential to building a home that can stand the tests that life brings.*

**TIP:** *Call attention to the main points of the first five sessions. Ask everyone to think silently about what they have learned, and especially about all that is involved in carrying out each of the actions required to build oneness in a marriage.*

*After a few moments of silence, ask, "If you are confident that under all circumstances you and your mate will always be able to carry out all these actions, mark 100 percent in the margin of your study guide. If you feel these actions are so totally out of character for you or your mate that you will probably never be able to do any of them, mark 0 percent. Or, estimate a realistic percentage somewhere in between those extremes." Allow a minute or two for people to mark a percentage.*

*Call for a show of hands of those who marked a figure below 100 percent. "How about below 90 percent? 80 percent?" When you get to a number where few people raise their hands, ask, "How many of you would be willing to fly in an airplane with less than an 80 percent chance of landing safely? What does it say to you about our chances for really developing oneness in our marriages if we anticipate a pretty high failure rate in carrying out the actions needed to develop oneness?"*

*Allow group members to respond to your questions, then introduce this session by inviting the group to look more closely at the two home builders Jesus talked about.*

*We have spent five sessions exploring God's blueprints for marriage—and putting them to work. In this session we will discover how God equips and empowers us to succeed in our desire to achieve oneness with our mate and with Him.*

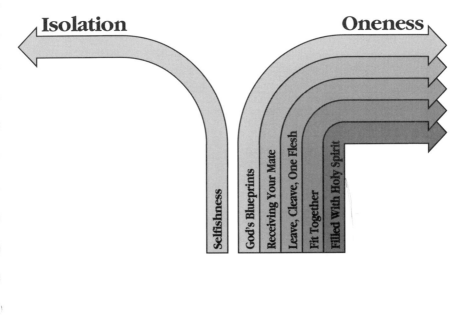

**Isolation**                                     **Oneness**

- Selfishness
- God's Blueprints
- Receiving Your Mate
- Leave, Cleave, One Flesh
- Fit Together
- Filled With Holy Spirit

# *Blueprints*

*(30-50 minutes)*

**COMMENT:** *It is impossible to fully cover all the truth regarding the Christian life in one session. The points covered here are intended to encourage individuals and couples to begin to experience the filling of the Holy Spirit as an essential step in a lifelong process of growth. For further study on this essential topic of Christian living there are some excellent small-group studies available from Campus Crusade for Christ.*

# A. THE HOUSE THE FLESH BUILDS
*(10-15 minutes)*

**1.** How well do you identify with Paul's lament (Romans 7:18, 19) of his inability to put into practice the truth he believed?

☐ I don't have that trouble at all.

☐ I fall short occasionally.

☐ He said what I feel!

☐ I'm even worse off than he was!

☐

> **TIP:** *Share your own reaction to Paul's plight. Ask, "How does this apply to two individuals who are seeking to build a Christian marriage?" (By themselves they are not capable.)*

**2.** Scripture frequently shows that even our best human efforts will not only fall short of success, but will actually end in destruction! What are some of the final results of your own desires and efforts ("the deeds of the flesh") as described in Galatians 5:16-21?

> **ANSWER:** *Immorality, impurity, sensuality, idolatry, sorcery, enmities, etc.*

> **OPTION:** *Ask a follow-up question: "After looking at these gross results, what do you see as the source of our problems in carrying out our good intentions in our lives and marriages?" (The flesh—our sinful nature—keeps us from doing the good things we know we should, for it is in opposition to the purposes of the Spirit [God's blueprints].)*

**3.** How are the "deeds of the flesh" sometimes made evident in your own marriage? (CAUTION: Don't embarrass your mate!)

> *TIP: Share an incident in your marriage when you failed to act on your own good intentions and produced a similarly negative result. Then ask three or four people in the group to briefly mention a comparable incident—without embarrassing their mates. When the sharing is completed, point out that Paul not only faced these same kinds of situations in his life; he also wrote about the solution to the problems by describing three categories into which all people fit.*

**4.** First Corinthians 2:14—3:3 describes three kinds of people:

 The Natural Person (2:14), who has not received Christ as Savior, does not understand spiritual truth and is in need of spiritual birth.

 The Spiritual Person (2:15,16), who has received Christ and wisely judges or appraises all of life according to God's Word.

 The Worldly or Carnal Person (3:1-3), who has received Christ but has not matured as a Christian and who is trying to live the Christian life by human effort.

Which description best fits you?

> *TIP: Briefly explain the three types of people illustrated by the three circles. If time permits, have a group member read the verses from 1 Corinthians which relate to each person. Ask everyone to privately write down which description best fits him or her.*

---

### HOMEBUILDERS PRINCIPLE #8:
## Only Spiritual Christians can have a hope of building godly homes.

---

*Important Note!*
*If you sense that anyone in your group is not a Christian, this might be a good time to take a few moments to explain the gospel. Refer to "The Four Spiritual Laws" section at the end of the leader's guides and study guides.*

*We suggest that you explain briefly how you can become a Christian and the differences that walking with Christ has made in your life. Then read through The Four Spiritual Laws presentation.*

*Also included at the end of the leader's guides and study guides is a longer explanation of the Holy Spirit and His power in our lives. Suggest to your group members that they read through this on their own.*

## B. THE HOUSE THE SPIRIT BUILDS
*(10-15 minutes)*

**COMMENT:** *In order for a home to weather the storms of life, its daily builder must be God. Jesus said it was to our advantage that He go to the Father, because He would send God's Holy Spirit (the "Helper" or "Comforter," the Third Person of the Trinity) to lead us, show us His ways and to empower us to represent Him to the world. (See John 14:26.) As two people build a relationship with each other, it is essential that they both yield to the Holy Spirit and allow Him to lead them in every facet of their marriage.*

*Be sure to define the Holy Spirit in reference to His role in Christian marriage: "He is God's personal presence in your marriage." Repeat the statement so each person can write it in the study guide.*

*OPTION:* *Ask, "Why do you think it is important for God to be present within a marriage?" (The purposes for which God designed marriage cannot be achieved apart from His presence. Intimacy with the Holy Spirit will release God's power in an individual and a marriage. Only He can enable a couple to overcome the barriers to His purpose of oneness.)*

**1.** Record below the characteristics listed in Galatians 5:22-26 of a person (or a home) who is yielding to God's Holy Spirit.

*ANSWER:* *Love, joy, peace, etc.*

**2.** Pick one part of the fruit of the Spirit that you most need in order to create oneness in your marriage:

How will this quality contribute to oneness in your marriage?

**3.** Every house has its builder (Hebrews 3:4). Do you feel your home is being built in the energy of the flesh or by the power of the Holy Spirit? Why?

If you are to build a godly home (one that shows forth God's character and attributes: His goodness, faithfulness, justice, love, etc.), you must do so through the power that God supplies. Human ability will never achieve godliness. In the previous session we saw the responsibilities for husbands and wives in Ephesians 5:22-31. This passage is preceded by the command to "be filled with the Spirit" (v.18).

*TIP:* *Ask each person to privately answer Question 3. Lead the group toward the next segment of this session: "We have seen that the Holy Spirit is an essential ingredient in a life and in a marriage. Yet many feel that living out marriage with the Holy Spirit is confusing or difficult, and they continue to struggle, attempting to build a strong marriage their own way, not really seeking to submit their lives and their relationship to God's control."*

---

**HOMEBUILDERS PRINCIPLE #9:**

**The home built by God requires both the husband and wife to yield to the Holy Spirit in every area of their lives.**

---

# C. THE HOLY SPIRIT IN YOUR LIFE
*(10-15 minutes)*

**1.** In Ephesians 5:18, Paul contrasts being "filled with the Spirit" with being "drunk with wine." What does this comparison say to you about what it means to be filled with the Spirit?

*ANSWER: This imagery conveys the idea of being controlled and empowered.*

■

**To** be filled (controlled and empowered) by the Holy Spirit is a process that will be repeated many times as you yield yourself to Christ and His authority over your life. It literally means "keep on being filled."

■

**2.** How then can you be filled with the Holy Spirit? The following are some beginning steps. (This process is further developed in the **HomeBuilders Project** to be done after this session.)

a. God will not fill an unclean vessel. What does 1 John 1:9 tell us to do about the sin in our lives? What does it mean to do this?

> ***ANSWER:*** *Confess it. Confession means to agree or admit that something is true. Confessing our sin involves telling God that we have sinned against Him. We must recognize that any relationship is damaged by selfishness (sin) in either partner. Oneness can only grow when selfishness is confronted and dealt with. When we sin, oneness with God is broken and must be dealt with before fellowship can be renewed.*

b. Knowing that we receive Christ by faith, how then do we allow Him to control our lives moment by moment? (Colossians 2:6)

> ***ANSWER:*** *The same way as we received Him—by faith. The phrase "walking in the Spirit" refers to the range of activities of an individual's life, conveying the idea of trusting daily in the power of the Spirit in contrast to depending on even the best of human intentions.*

c. What is faith and why is it important in being filled with the Spirit? (Hebrews 11:1,6)

> ***ANSWER:*** *Faith is assurance that something—or Someone—is true, no matter what we feel or what the*

*circumstances are. Without faith in God we cannot please Him, for then we are depending on ourselves or some other source rather than on Him and His Word. We exercise faith when we trustingly yield control of our lives to Him, rather than trying to succeed through our own best efforts. While feelings are usually involved, they are not the basis for assurance, since they are so easily changed by circumstances.*

d. Does God desire to fill you with His Holy Spirit? (Ephesians 5:18)

**ANSWER:** *He would only command us to be filled with the Spirit if He desired it for us.*

e. What has God promised you? (1 John 5:14,15)

**ANSWER:** *God promises in His Word to answer any request that is in accord with His will. Since He has specifically stated that it is His will to fill us with His Spirit, you can be assured that if you pray for Him to fill you, He will honor your prayer.*

f. Look again at the three circles in part A. Which one represents your life now? Which one do you want to represent your life?

**TIP:** *Ask each person to privately write his or her answer to the first question. Then ask everyone to privately write his or her answer to the second one, also.*

*Point out that this session has established several essential facts about being filled with the Holy Spirit:*

*It is a command.*
*It is a promise God will honor.*

> *It is essential in building a life and a marriage upon the Rock, able to withstand life's onslaughts.*
>
> *Remind the group of the earlier discussion of the wise builder and the third little pig: the pig was depending on his own planning and effort; the wise builder was listening to and obeying God's Word.*

g. After considering these truths, once again distinguish the difference between the wise man and foolish man in Matthew 7. What steps do you need to take to insure that your house is being built upon the Rock?

> ***ANSWER:*** *Confess your sin. In faith yield your life to His control instead of your own control. Ask Him to fill you with His Spirit. Obey God and His Word.*

h. Will you ask God to fill you and control you with His Spirit?

> ***TIP:*** *Ask each person to write his or her answer.*

i. Why not take a moment right now and bow in prayer, asking God to empower you with His Spirit?

> ***TIP:*** *Lead the group in silent prayer. Allow 60-90 seconds for this process. Do not be afraid of the silence— it is a time of evaluation and, most importantly, response to God.*

**3.** If you confessed your sins, yielded your life to Him and asked God to fill you with His Spirit, then did He fill you with His Spirit? How can you know?

> ***ANSWER:*** *Yes. Refer back to God's statement of His will in Ephesians 5:18 and His promise to grant requests which are in accord with His will. Faith in His integrity and His Word is the basis for our assurance.*
>
> ***OPTION:*** *If you contacted someone earlier in the week about sharing his experience with being filled with the Spirit, this would be a good time to have him or her talk.*

# Construction

*(15-20 minutes)*

*These **Construction** exercises are different from those in earlier sessions in that they focus very pointedly on each spouse's spiritual condition. Whether a couple shares a commitment to obeying God's Word, or one is committed and the other is not, or neither is committed, responding to these questions will help them nudge each other in the direction of positive growth in the spiritual areas of their lives.*

**1.** What is the admonition of Galatians 6:7-9, and how can we apply it in building our home?

**2.** Practically speaking, my greatest hindrance to walking in the power of the Holy Spirit is...

**3.** How can we help and encourage each other to walk in the power of the Holy Spirit?

**4.** In what practical, everyday situations would the power of the Holy Spirit make a difference in our marriage (i.e., communication, sex, in-laws, roles, conflict resolution, acceptance, etc.)? What one thing can we do to see this difference realized?

> *TIP: When the couples are finished, have them return to the group and ask each to share a response to one* **Construction** *item. Summarize this sharing by reminding them of these central points about the Christian life:*
>
> *Walking in the Holy Spirit is by faith, not feelings.*
>
> *Walking in the Holy Spirit is a subjective experience which is objectified (confirmed) by the Word of God.*
>
> *Walking in the Holy Spirit requires a sensitive and submissive spirit, continually yielding control to Him.*

## Make a Date

*Remind the couples to make a date to complete* **HomeBuilders Project #6** *this week. Explain that this project goes more in depth about dealing with sin and being filled with the Spirit. While it requires 60-90 minutes to complete, this project can have the greatest impact on each person's life and marriage.*

Make a date with your mate to meet in the next few days to complete **HomeBuilders Project #6**. Your leader will ask at the next session for you to share one thing from this experience.

_____   _____   _____
Date                   Time                   Location

# Recommended Reading

**The Holy Spirit**, by Bill Bright.

The door to life's greatest adventure—the walk of faith, purpose and power—can be unlocked through the strength and guidance of the Holy Spirit. Find out who He is, His purpose and His relationship to you. Basic principles for spiritual growth and ministry effectiveness.

**Staying Close**, by Dennis Rainey.

Chapter 13—"The Power for Oneness"—discusses the role of the Holy Spirit in strengthening your marriage.

**Transferable Concepts for Powerful Living**, by Bill Bright.

1. *How to Be Sure You Are a Christian*
2. *How to Experience God's Love and Forgiveness*
3. *How to Be Filled with the Spirit*
4. *How to Walk in the Spirit*

These booklets explain the "how-to's" of consistent, successful Christian living. Excellent for personal enrichment and as gifts for growing Christians.

*Conclude with prayer and a time of fellowship.*

# HOMEBUILDERS PROJECT #6

Learning to live the Christian life is an ongoing process. The following project will aid you in your discovery of the great adventures of daily walking in the power of the Holy Spirit. Building a home that reflects God's character is a matter of choices—choices that are made by faith, trusting that God's Word is true and that He will do what He promises in Scripture.

## As a Couple: 5-10 minutes

Share with each other two or three things that really spoke to your needs from Session Six.

# Individually: 60-90 minutes

## A. We Must Desire to Walk in the Spirit

1. What does Matthew 5:6 teach about a prerequisite for walking in the power of the Holy Spirit?

2. Why is the desire to be Christlike so important?

3. Proverbs 2:1-5 speaks of a commitment and desire for knowing God. List applications to your marriage that you can discern from this passage.

## B. We Must Continually Confess Our Sin

1. Sin plagues us in our relationship with God. It alienates us from Him (Proverbs 15:9) and produces "death" (Romans 6:23). Since sin breaks our fellowship with God, it is necessary to restore that relationship when we find that we have been displeasing Him. What does the Bible say to do when fellowship with God has been broken (1 John 1:5-10)?

2. To confess means "to agree with another." We agree with God that our actions or attitudes are wrong. We then repent, turning from these sins and back to God, thanking Him for Christ's death on the cross for all our sins. Why is repentance crucial to our confession?

3. Read Colossians 2:13,14. When we confess our sin before God, should we:

☐ beg for God's forgiveness?

☐ thank Him that the penalty has been paid and that He has already forgiven us?

**NOTE:** An exercise that hundreds of thousands of Christians have found meaningful is to take a separate sheet of paper and spend time alone with God, asking Him to reveal any sin that is unconfessed before Him. The following steps are recommended:

1. Title the page, "For God's Eyes Only." Prayerfully list on the page actions and attitudes that are contrary to God's Word and purposes. Focus on areas that affect your mate.
2. After 15-20 minutes, write the words of 1 John 1:9 across your list of sins, thanking God for His absolute forgiveness of all that you have done in the past, present and future. Thank Him for sending His Son to the cross to die for your sin.
3. It may be necessary and appropriate for you to also confess to your mate any attitudes or actions that have been harmful to him/her. Caution: Do not dredge up something from the past that would be more than your mate can handle. Seek wise counsel and avoid dropping any "atomic bombs." There is a significant difference between confessing something that your mate knows about and "getting something off your chest" that makes you feel better but becomes a severe problem to your mate.
4. Destroy the page and continue your study on being filled with the Holy Spirit.

4. When you are tempted to sin, what does God's Word promise in 1 Corinthians 10:13?

5. As a Christian, you have power over sin. Read Romans 6:1-18 and answer the following questions:

a. What happened to your sinful nature when you received Christ (v.6)?

b. According to verse 11, what must you do?

c. According to verses 16 and 17, what choices must you make?

d. Have you been freed from sin?     □ Yes     □ No

Are you still a slave to sin?     □ Yes     □ No

To what are you to be a slave?

e. What do you need to do as a result of studying these verses about the freedom Christ has given you?

## C. We Must Yield Ownership of Our Life to Jesus Christ

1. What do Romans 6:12-14; 12:1,2 tell you to do?

2. Have you ever given Jesus Christ complete ownership of your life?     ☐ Yes   ☐ No

   If not, would you like to right now?     ☐ Yes   ☐ No

   Simply bow in prayer and acknowledge His authority over your life. Give Him the "title deed." Write out your commitment to Him in the space below. Sign and date your statement.

_____     _____
              Signature                                    Date

## D. We Must by Faith Claim the Filling of the Holy Spirit

1. Check each statement as you read:

   ☐ **His Command:** Be filled with the Spirit (Ephesians 5:18).

   ☐ **His Promise:** He will always answer when we pray according to His will (1 John 5:14,15).

2. Is it God's will that you be filled with the Holy Spirit?

   ☐ Yes     ☐ No   (Review #1 if you are not sure.)

3. When you pray in faith and ask God to fill you, will He do it?

☐ Yes      ☐ No

How do you know? (Check #1 again.)

4. Why not express right now your obedience and faith to God?

> Dear Father, I need You. I admit that I have been directing my own life and I have sinned against You. I thank You that You have forgiven my sins through Christ's death on the cross for me. I now invite Christ to be Lord over all my life. Fill me with the Holy Spirit as You commanded me to be filled, and as You promised in your Word that You would do if I ask in faith. As an expression of my faith, I now thank You for directing my life and for filling me with the Holy Spirit. Amen.

If this prayer expressed the desire of your heart, then simply bow in prayer and trust God to empower you with the Holy Spirit **right now**.

## Interact as a Couple: 15-20 minutes

Share with one another the decision you have made in response to this study. Your relationship with one another will benefit as you openly talk about your spiritual commitments—as well as confiding any questions or struggles. Close your time together by praying for one another.

Be ready to share with the group one specific experience from this project: perhaps an instance when you allowed the Holy Spirit to fill you in your marriage relationship or one area in which you have recognized a struggle in yielding to His control.

Remember to bring your calendar for **Make a Date**
to the next session.

# BUILDING A LEGACY

## OBJECTIVES

You will help your group members build an eternal legacy as you guide them to:

- Compare a worldly legacy with a godly legacy;
- Identify the spiritual and physical legacies a marriage can leave;
- Evaluate the direction of their lives and marriages and determine the type of legacy they want to leave; and
- Discuss with their mate specific actions they can take to build a godly legacy.

## OVERALL COMMENTS

1. It is crucial that you approach this seventh session as an opportunity to encourage couples to take specific steps beyond this series to keep their marriage growing. While this HomeBuilders Couples Series has great value in itself, people are likely to gradually return to their previous patterns of living unless they commit to a plan for carrying on the progress made. Continuing effort is required for people to initiate and maintain new directions in their marriage.

   FamilyLife of Campus Crusade for Christ is committed to changing the destiny of the family and providing quality resources to build distinctively Christian marriages. The HomeBuilders Couples Series is designed to take a couple

through essential components important to building committed Christian marriages and Christian families. Several studies
are now available, and many more are planned for future
availability.

Those available now are:

*Building Your Marriage:* The basic introduction of God's
principles for marriage.

*Building Your Mate's Self-Esteem:* A unique plan of building
blocks to strengthen your mate's self-image.

*Building Teamwork in Your Marriage:* Designed for men
and women to explore God's purpose for their lives, their
roles, responsibilities and differentness.

*Mastering Your Money in Your Marriage:* Developed to
help couples identify and grapple with the whole concept of
a biblical approach to finances and to provide practical guide-
lines in planning personal finances.

*Resolving Conflict in Your Marriage:* Couples can't avoid
conflict in marriage but they can learn to handle their conflicts
in a way that brings them together instead of driving them
further apart.

As you prepare this session, prayerfully consider challenging the couples in your group to either participate in another
study or to start their own group.

Either commit to participate in another study, such as
*Building Your Mate's Self-Esteem;* or begin your own group of
couples to study *Building Your Marriage.*

2. If your group includes childless couples, focus most of your
   attention during this session on spiritual descendants rather
   than physical descendants. Also, if there are couples whose
   children are grown or nearly grown and who are not serving
   Christ, encourage those parents that God is still able to over-
   rule any mistakes made in earlier years. He can use parents'
   past failures for His good. Encourage these parents to confess
   their errors to God—and to their children; this can be a powerful means of restoring relationships and communication.
   Urge them to focus on the remaining years to use every
   teachable moment with their children to share their present
   values and relationship with Christ.

3. Ask how many did the **HomeBuilders Project** from the last
   session. Ask for a show of hands of those who did the proj-

ect. Do not chide those who did not but encourage them to complete it, and if needed make up unfinished projects. Have two people share (the purpose of this is for accountability). Congratulate those who did and underscore the importance of doing the project for each session.

God's purpose for marriage goes beyond intimacy, sharing romantic times together and achieving oneness. Marriage is meant to be a couple's locking arms together to influence their world and future generations with the gospel of Jesus Christ.

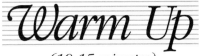

*(10-15 minutes)*

We have been exposed to much about God's plan for our marriages so far in our study.

**1.** Mark the concept that you have found to be most significant in your marriage:

☐ We must deal with the threats to oneness that result in isolation.

☐ We must understand God's blueprints as shown in five purposes for marriage (Mirror, Multiply, Manage, Mutually Complete, Model).

☐ We build a solid foundation by receiving our mate as a gift from God.

☐ We construct according to God's plan when we leave, cleave and become one flesh, resulting in total transparency with our mate.

☐ We fit together with our mate when we commit to fulfilling our roles defined in the blueprint of Scripture.

☐ We are empowered by the Holy Spirit to carry out these principles and purposes.

**2.** What do you feel is the most important change you have made thus far in your marriage as a result of this series?

> **TIP:** *The answers to Point 1 may touch on Question 2. Share your own answer to set an example of openness about specific changes in actions or attitudes. Stating these changes in front of the group will help to solidify them in people's minds as important things to continue.*
>
> *Call for a show of hands of any who marked the first statement (We must deal with the threats to oneness that result in isolation). Ask those who raise their hands to tell what they have found to be significant in that concept. Continue similarly with the other statements listed.*

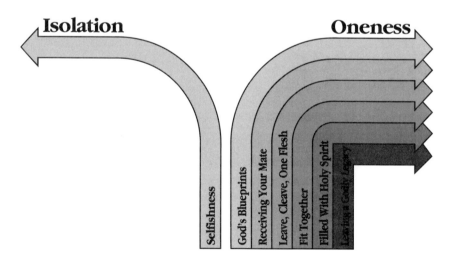

Isolation           Oneness

Selfishness | God's Blueprints | Receiving Your Mate | Leave, Cleave, One Flesh | Fit Together | Filled With Holy Spirit | Leaving a Godly Legacy

**We** have learned many things about how to let the Lord build our house. Now we need to learn that "building the house" is not an end in itself.

**Although** God is deeply interested in our fulfillment as individuals within marriage, He does not give us a "great and satisfying" marriage just so we can have a warm and wonderful relationship with another person. Scripture teaches that in marriage we are to experience growth and acceptance in order to enable us to reach beyond the doors of our home to a neighborhood and a world in great need.

**God's** heart of love is virtually breaking over people who have not yet received His forgiveness through His Son Jesus Christ. Reconciling people to Himself is God's desire for every individual and for every marriage. You and your mate and those you influence for Christ, including your children, are all a part of God's purpose for planet Earth.

**We** have already seen that oneness with God and with our mate is necessary for overcoming isolation in our marriages. The oneness we are establishing in our homes is also enabling us to reach out to others afflicted by isolation.

**A couple** that is working together to meet needs beyond their own front door will leave a spiritual legacy that will outlive them. In so doing, they will discover that their marriage is thriving as they give their lives away in ministering to the needs of others.

---

### HOMEBUILDERS PRINCIPLE #10:

## The heritage you were handed is not as important as the legacy you will leave.

---

# Blueprints
### (30-45 minutes)

## A. UNDERSTANDING OUR HERITAGE
### (10-15 minutes)

**1.** What comes to mind when you think of a "heritage" or a "legacy"?

> ***ANSWER:*** *Something that is passed on from one person to another, an inheritance, birthright, etc.*

**2.** There are other types of legacies which people leave. List as many different kinds as you can.

> ***TIP:*** *Allow a minute for group members to write, then ask for answers.*

**3.** To what extent is the legacy a person leaves a statement of his or her true values? Explain why this would be so.

> ***ANSWER:*** *That which outlives a person defines to others what that person really valued.*

**4.** Describe the heritage your parents left to you and the values it represents.

> ***TIP:*** *Give your group members some time to think of their answers and write down some notes. Then invite volunteers to read aloud what they have written. Allow plenty of time for sharing here.*

**5.** Look up the following Scriptures and write down words or phrases that describe the legacy God desires you to leave.

Deuteronomy 6:1,2,5-7

> ***ANSWER:*** *Fear the Lord, keep His laws, love the Lord, know His Word.*

Joshua 24:14,15

> ***ANSWER:*** *Family commitment to fear and serve God.*

Psalm 112:1,2

> ***ANSWER:*** *Fear the Lord and delight in His commands.*

Proverbs 4:10-15

> ***ANSWER:*** *Wisdom, uprightness.*

2 Timothy 1:5

> ***ANSWER:*** *Sincere faith.*

3 John 4

> ***ANSWER:*** *Walking in the truth.*

Leaving a godly legacy will ultimately be different for every individual. The true test in leaving a godly legacy is an individual's or a couples faithful fulfillment of God's mission through the stewardship of time, talents and treasure. A godly legacy can be partially measured in the character of the descendants who have been spiritually influenced by a person's life.

---

### HOMEBUILDERS PRINCIPLE #11:
## The legacy you leave is determined by the life you live.

---

# B. How to Leave a Legacy That Will Outlive You *(10-15 minutes)*

According to 2 Timothy 2:2 and Psalm 78:3-8, you can leave spiritual as well as physical descendants.

*TIP: Have the group look up those two verses to see what they have to say about leaving spiritual descendants:*

*Second Timothy 2:2 stresses the importance of finding faithful men to build your life into, with the goal of helping them do the same with other faithful men.*

*Psalm 78:3-8 talks about teaching our children about the things of God.*

**1.** How do you leave a spiritual legacy? (Matthew 28:19,20).

*ANSWER: By reaching out to those in our world in order to make disciples.*

**2.** According to Deuteronomy 6:4-9, how do you leave a godly legacy through your influence on your children, your physical descendants?

*ANSWER: A godly legacy is obviously more than just physical reproduction. God's purpose is not just more people, but to "multiply a godly legacy." Deuteronomy 6 shows that this is accomplished as parents tell and show God's truth to their children in the midst of everyday living.*

# AN EXAMPLE OF LEAVING A SPIRITUAL LEGACY

**As** you near the completion of this study, you have become part of the godly legacy from a remarkable single woman who left no physical descendants. Humanly speaking, this series might never have been created if it had not been that Dr. Henrietta Mears befriended a young couple in the early years of their spiritual growth. Bill Bright, founder of Campus Crusade for Christ, and his wife Vonette were strongly influenced by Dr. Mears.

**Many** other individuals and organizations are part of the spiritual legacy left by Dr. Mears, including Billy Graham, Donn Moomaw (Former President Reagan's pastor at Bel Air Presbyterian Church), Richard Halverson (Chaplain of the United States Senate), Gospel Light Publications (a major producer of Bible study resources and Christian literature), Forest Home (one of the largest Christian conference centers in the United States), and Gospel Literature International (GLINT—a service organization aiding in the translation of Christian literature throughout the world).

**If** you have grown spiritually through The HomeBuilders Couples Series, then you are a part of the spiritual legacy of Henrietta Mears. Do you believe that God could still be multiplying **your** spiritual legacy three generations from now?

*TIP: Have someone read aloud the story of Henrietta Mears. During your discussion, encourage parents to be aware that the results of faithful teaching cannot always be seen at present, but we can know if we are being faithful in teaching our children and we can tell if we are growing in our ability to communicate our faith to them and to others. Point out that children are messengers we send to a time we cannot see— and no project a couple undertakes has more potential for long range impact than faithfully teaching God's truth to their children.*

---

HOMEBUILDERS PRINCIPLE #12:
**Your marriage should leave
a legacy of love that will
influence future generations.**

---

# C. MOTIVATION FOR LEAVING A GODLY LEGACY *(10-15 minutes)*

**1.** What in the following verses motivates you to leave a godly legacy?

Matthew 28:19,20

> ***ANSWER:*** *Jesus commanded it.*

Romans 1:16

> ***ANSWER:*** *We are not to be ashamed of the gospel and its power to save.*

Romans 8:35-39

> ***ANSWER:*** *No difficulty can separate us from Christ's love and protection; thus, we are assured that we will succeed when we depend on Him.*

Ephesians 2:10

> ***ANSWER:*** *God created us to do good.*

1 Peter 3:9-15

*ANSWER:* *God called us to be blessed; therefore, we are to pursue good, even when facing trouble.*

2 Peter 3:9-15

*ANSWER:* *God will end this present world; His patience is our opportunity.*

**2.** Read 1 Corinthians 3:10-15 and contrast the final results of a worldly and godly legacy.

*ANSWER:* *A worldly heritage—even the best of this material world will be destroyed. A godly heritage— God will reward those who build according to His blueprints.*

**3.** Describe the legacy you would leave if your life ended tonight:

*TIP:* *Instruct each person to silently write an answer to Item 3. Ask for volunteers to share their answers. This could be a very positive time for many who have not yet yielded to Christ in your group.*

# Construction

*(20-30 minutes)*

*This* **Construction** *section pushes couples into some heavy evaluation of the legacy they are currently working on and the legacy they want to pass on. This will require more time than the session allows; if time does not allow couples to com-*

*plete this section during the session, they may do so when they work on the **HomeBuilders Project**.*

*Before you have the couples meet by themselves, briefly share your response to one or two **Construction** items, giving group members an idea of how to proceed (e.g., "Values—I really do value people and God's work more than material goods. Schedule—I don't spend enough time on what I claim to value most...").*

*Next, explain the options under Question 3, encouraging each couple to either commit to something that will help them leave a godly legacy. Have them plan tonight (or at least this week) the specific steps they will take to carry out the action chosen. If any couples feel these options are not possible for them at this time, encourage them to think of another action plan which will fit their situation and help them continue to grow in fulfilling God's purposes in and through their marriage.*

*As couples talk, be available to answer questions and to periodically announce how much time is left.*

*Gather the couples back together to conclude the session and the series by inviting each couple to share their response to one item.*

**1.** What do you want your legacy to be? What people do you need to influence for God? What are some tasks in your church you are gifted to tackle? What project should you support?

**2.** Evaluate the type of legacy your marriage is now leaving in the following areas. Focus on one or two areas.

Love for People

Values

Schedule and Priorities

Sharing Christ with Friends/Associates

Finances/Possessions

Leadership

Children

**3.** What one specific action do you need to take to better use your marriage to leave a godly legacy? Consider:

☐ Commit to participate in other studies of The Home-Builders Couples Series.

☐ Gather another group of couples and lead them in studying *Building Your Marriage.*

☐ Begin weekly family nights—teaching your children about Christ.

☐ Host an evangelistic dinner party—invite your non-Christian friends to your home and as a couple share your faith in Christ and the forgiveness of His gospel.

☐ Share the good news of Jesus Christ with neighborhood children.

☐

For information on any of the above ministry opportunities, contact your local church, or write:

FamilyLife
P.O. Box 23840
Little Rock, AR 72221-3840
(501) 223-8663

**4.** Most people seek to leave a legacy that will honor them. What does Psalm 45:16,17 add to this goal? How can you and your mate make this a reality in your marriage and family?

# Make a Date

Make a date with your mate to meet in the next few days to complete **HomeBuilders Project #7**. Your leader will ask at the next session for you to share one thing from this experience.

| | | |
|---|---|---|
| Date | Time | Location |

# Recommended Reading

**Staying Close**, by Dennis Rainey

"A Mother's Influence," "A Word to Dads," "Your Family Can Make the Difference," and "How to Become a HomeBuilder" are recommended chapters for this session.

**Dream Big: The Henrietta Mears Story**, edited by Earl Roe.

*Lead the group in a time of prayer for each other's continued growth in oneness.*

*Invite the group to remain for refreshments and informal conversations about what each couple's next step will be for continued growth and for influencing their world for Christ.*

## HOMEBUILDERS PROJECT #7

After completing this project, send a **copy** to your group leader within 7 to 10 days.

### Individually: 20-30 minutes

Write out a description of the legacy you desire to leave:

a. to your physical descendants—your children, if God so blesses:

b. to your spiritual descendants—those you lead to Christ and disciple:

## Interact as a Couple: 20-30 minutes

**1.** Compare your descriptions, then make one common description of the legacy you both desire to leave:

a. for your physical descendants

b. for your spiritual descendants

**2.** Copy or type your statement and place it at work or home as a reminder of your objective. You may want to mount or frame it.

**3.** Discuss options that are available to you (individually and as a couple) to equip and assist you to leave a godly legacy (local church, Bible study group, outreach event).

**4.** Write one major objective you wish to accomplish this year in helping you:

a. leave a godly line of physical descendants:

b. leave a godly line of spiritual descendants:

**NOTE:** *After the group members finish this last session, please encourage them to fill out the evaluation at the end of the study. They can then send them in individually or you could, as the group leader, collect all evaluations and send them in for the group.*

*A Personal Word from the Author*

*Like an exhausted runner who has just completed and won the race, you may feel both exhilaration and relief upon completion of your HomeBuilders Couples Series study. Regardless, I want to thank you for your hours of preparation, prayer and ministry in the lives of others. There is nothing quite like being used by God to spiritually strengthen another person's life. You have just experienced that satisfaction. I want to add my voice to those in your group to say thank-you for your part in leaving a significant spiritual legacy. You are a part of a rapidly growing movement that is doing something about the rapid decay of the family.*

*If you are like me you probably learned more, grew more and benefited more than those whom you led. But you also probably made a difference in some very valuable people's lives. Thank you for your part in changing the destiny of families.*

*May God bless you.*

*DENNIS RAINEY*

# WHERE DO YOU GO FROM HERE?

It is my prayer that you have benefited greatly from this study in The HomeBuilders Couples Series. I hope that your marriage will continue to grow as you both submit your lives to Jesus Christ and build according to His blueprints.

I also hope that you will begin reaching out to strengthen other marriages in your community and local church. Your pastor needs lay couples, like yourselves, who are committed to building Christian marriages. One of my favorite World War II stories illustrates this point very clearly.

The year was 1940. The French Army had just collapsed under the siege of Hitler's onslaught. The Dutch had folded, overwhelmed by the Nazi regime. The Belgians had surrendered. And the British Army was trapped on the coast of France in the channel port of Dunkirk.

Two hundred and twenty thousand of Britain's finest young men seemed doomed to die, turning the English Channel red with their blood. The Fuehrer's troops, only miles away in the hills of France, didn't realize how close to victory they actually were.

Any rescue seemed feeble and futile in the time remaining. A "thin" British Navy—"the professionals"— told King George VI that at best they could save 17,000 troops. The House of Commons was warned to prepare for "hard and heavy tidings."

Politicians were paralyzed. The king was powerless. And the allies could only watch as spectators from a distance. Then as the doom of the British Army seemed imminent, a strange fleet appeared on the horizon of the English Channel; the wildest assortment of boats perhaps ever assembled in history. Trawlers, tugs, scows, fishing sloops, lifeboats, pleasure craft, smacks and coasters, sailboats, an island ferry by the name of *Gracie Fields*, even the *Endeavor*, the America's Cup challenger, came, as well as the London fire-brigade flotilla. Each ship was manned by civilian volunteers—English fathers sailing to rescue Britain's exhausted, bleeding sons.

William Manchester writes in his novel, *The Last Lion*, that even today what happened in 1940 in less than 24 hours seems like a miracle—not only were all of the British soldiers rescued, but 118,000 Allied troops as well.

Today many Christian homes are much like those troops of Dunkirk. Pressured, trapped and demoralized, they need help. Your help. The Christian community may be much like England—we stand waiting for politicians, professionals, even for our pastor to step in and save the family. But the problem is much larger than all of those combined can solve.

With the highest divorce rate of any nation on earth, we need an all-out rescue effort by American men and women "sailing" to rescue the exhausted and wounded family casualties. No paid professionals, just common couples with faith in an uncommon God. For too long, those of us in full-time vocational ministry have robbed lay men and women, like you, of the privilege and responsibility of influencing others.

Possibly this study has indeed been used to "light the torch" of your spiritual lives. Perhaps it was already burning and this provided more fuel. Regardless, may we challenge you to invest your lives in others?

You and other couples around the United States can team

together to build thousands of marriages and families. By starting a HomeBuilders group you will not only strengthen other marriages; you will also see your marriage grow as you teach these principles to others.

The following are some practical ways you can make a difference in families today:

1. Gather a group of couples (four to seven) and lead them through the seven sessions of this HomeBuilders study, *Building Your Marriage.* (Why not consider challenging others in your church or community to form new HomeBuilders groups?)
2. Commit to participate in another study in The HomeBuilders Couples Series.
3. Begin weekly family nights—teaching your children about Christ, the Bible and the Christian life.
4. Show the film, *JESUS,* on video as an evangelistic outreach in your neighborhood. For more information, write to:

> Inspirational Media
> 30012 Ivy Glenn Dr., Suite 200
> Laguna Niguel, CA. 92677

5. Host an evangelistic dinner party—invite your non-Christian friends to your home and as a couple share your faith in Christ and the forgiveness of His gospel.
6. Share the good news of Jesus Christ with neighborhood children.
7. If you have attended the FamilyLife Marriage Conference, why not assist your pastor in counseling pre-marrieds using the material you received?

For more information on any of the above ministry opportunities, contact your local church, or write:

> FamilyLife
> P.O. Box 23840
> Little Rock, AR 72221-3840
> (501) 223-8663

## ABOUT THE AUTHOR:

Dennis Rainey is director of FamilyLife. A graduate of the University of Arkansas and Dallas Theological Seminary, he joined the staff of Campus Crusade for Christ International in 1970. He is general editor of The HomeBuilders Couples Series.

Dennis has also written *Staying Close; Pulling Weeds, Planting Seeds;* and *Building Your Marriage* of The HomeBuilders Couples Series. Together Dennis and his wife, Barbara, have written *The Questions Book for Marriage Intimacy* and *Building Your Mate's Self-Esteem.* They are parents of six children—Ashley, Benjamin, Samuel, Rebecca, Deborah and Laura. They live near Little Rock, Arkansas.

# THE FOUR SPIRITUAL LAWS*

Just as there are physical laws that govern the physical universe, so are there spiritual laws that govern your relationship with God.

> **LAW ONE: God loves you and offers a wonderful plan for your life.**

## God's Love
"For God so loved the world, that He gave His only begotten Son, that whoever believes in Him should not perish, but have eternal life" (John 3:16).

## God's Plan
(Christ speaking) "I came that they might have life, and might have it abundantly" (that it might be full and meaningful) (John 10:10).

Why is it that most people are not experiencing the abundant life? Because...

> **LAW TWO: Man is sinful and separated from God. Therefore, he cannot know and experience God's love and plan for his life.**

## Man Is Sinful
"For all have sinned and fall short of the glory of God" (Romans 3:23).

Man was created to have fellowship with God; but, because of his stubborn self-will, chose to go his own independent way, and fellowship with God was broken. This self-will, characterized by an attitude of active rebellion or passive indifference, is evidence of what the Bible calls sin.

## Man Is Separated

"For the wages of sin is death" (spiritual separation from God) (Romans 6:23).

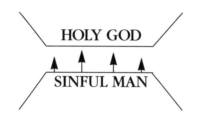

This diagram illustrates that God is holy and man is sinful. A great gulf separates the two. The arrows illustrate that man is continually trying to reach God and the abundant life through his own efforts, such as a good life, philosophy, or religion.

The third law explains the only way to bridge this gulf...

> **LAW THREE: Jesus Christ is God's only provision for man's sin. Through Him you can know and experience God's love and plan for your life.**

## He Died in Our Place

"But God demonstrates His own love toward us, in that while we were yet sinners, Christ died for us" (Romans 5:8).

## He Rose from the Dead

"Christ died for our sins . . . He was buried . . . He was raised on the third day according to the Scriptures . . . He appeared to [Peter], then to the twelve. After that He appeared to more than five hundred . . ." (1 Corinthians 15:3-6).

## He Is the Only Way to God

"Jesus said to him, 'I am the way, and the truth, and the life; no one comes to the Father, but through Me'" (John 14:6).

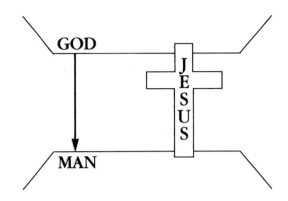

This diagram illustrates that God has bridged the gulf that separates us from Him by sending His Son, Jesus Christ, to die on the cross in our place to pay the penalty for our sins.

It is not enough just to know these three laws . . .

---

**LAW FOUR: We must individually receive Jesus Christ as Savior and Lord; then we can know and experience God's love and plan for our lives.**

---

## We Must Receive Christ
"But as many as received Him, to them He gave the right to become children of God, even to those who believe in His name" (John 1:12).

## We Receive Christ Through Faith
"For by grace you have been saved through faith; and that not of yourselves, it is the gift of God; not as a result of works, that no one should boast" (Ephesians 2:8,9).

## When We Receive Christ, We Experience a New Birth
(Read John 3:1-8.)

## We Receive Christ by Personal Invitation
(Christ is speaking) "Behold, I stand at the door and knock; if any one hears My voice and opens the door, I will come in to him" (Revelation 3:20).

Receiving Christ involves turning to God from self (repentance) and trusting Christ to come into our lives to forgive our sins and to make us the kind of people He wants us to be. Just to agree intellectually that Jesus Christ is the Son of God and that He died on the cross for our sins is not enough. Nor is it enough to have an emotional experience. We receive Jesus Christ by faith, as an act of the will.

These two circles represent two kinds of lives:

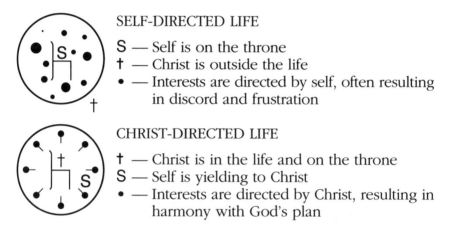

SELF-DIRECTED LIFE

S — Self is on the throne
† — Christ is outside the life
• — Interests are directed by self, often resulting in discord and frustration

CHRIST-DIRECTED LIFE

† — Christ is in the life and on the throne
S — Self is yielding to Christ
• — Interests are directed by Christ, resulting in harmony with God's plan

Which circle best represents your life?
Which circle would you like to have represent your life?
The following explains how you can receive Christ:

## You Can Receive Christ Right Now By Faith Through Prayer
(Prayer is talking with God.)

God knows your heart and is not so concerned with your words as He is with the attitude of your heart. The following is a suggested prayer:

> *Lord Jesus, I need You. Thank You for dying on the cross for my sins. I open the door of my life and receive You as my Savior and Lord. Thank You for forgiving my sins and giving me eternal life. Make me the kind of person You want me to be.*

Does this prayer express the desire of your heart?
If it does, pray this prayer right now, and Christ will come into your life, as He promised.

# HAVE YOU MADE THE WONDERFUL DISCOVERY OF THE SPIRIT-FILLED LIFE?*

Every day can be an exciting adventure for the Christian who knows the reality of being filled with the Holy Spirit and who lives constantly, moment by moment, under His gracious control. The Bible tells us that there are three kinds of people:

**1.** NATURAL MAN (one who has not received Christ)

"But a natural man does not accept the things of the Spirit of God; for they are foolishness to him, and he cannot understand them, because they are spiritually appraised" (1 Corinthians 2:14).

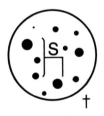

SELF-DIRECTED LIFE
S— Ego or finite self is on the throne
†— Christ is outside the life
•— Interests are controlled by self, often resulting in discord and frustration

**2.** SPIRITUAL MAN (one who is controlled and empowered by the Holy Spirit)

"But he who is spiritual appraises all things..." (1 Corinthians 2:15).

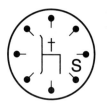

CHRIST-DIRECTED LIFE
**†** — Christ on the throne of the life
**S** — Ego or self is dethroned
**•** — Interests are under control of infinite God, resulting in harmony with God's plan

**3.** CARNAL MAN (one who has received Christ, but who lives in defeat because he trusts in his own efforts to live the Christian life)

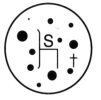

SELF-DIRECTED LIFE
**S** — Ego or finite self is on the throne
**†** — Christ is dethroned
**•** — Interests controlled by self, often resulting in discord and frustration

"And I, brethren, could not speak to you as to spiritual men, but as to carnal men, as to babes in Christ. I gave you milk to drink, not solid food; for you were not yet able to receive it. Indeed, even now you are not yet able, for you are still carnal. For since there is jealousy and strife among you, are you not fleshly, and are you not walking like mere men?" (1 Corinthians 3:1-3).

# A. GOD HAS PROVIDED FOR US AN ABUNDANT AND FRUITFUL CHRISTIAN LIFE

Jesus said, "I came that they might have life, and might have it abundantly" (John 10:10).

"I am the vine, you are the branches; he who abides in Me, and I in him, he bears much fruit; for apart from Me you can do nothing" (John 15:5).

"But the fruit of the Spirit is love, joy, peace, patience, kindness, goodness, faithfulness, gentleness, self-control; against such things there is no law" (Galatians 5:22,23).

"But you shall receive power when the Holy Spirit has come upon you; and you shall be My witnesses both in Jerusalem, and in all Judea and Samaria, and even to the remotest part of the earth" (Acts 1:8).

### THE SPIRITUAL MAN
Some Personal Traits that Result from Trusting God:

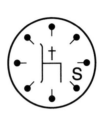

Christ-centered
Empowered by the Holy Spirit
Introduces others to Christ
Effective prayer life
Understands God's Word
Trusts God
Obeys God

Love
Joy
Peace
Patience
Kindness
Goodness
Faithfulness

The degree to which these traits are manifested in the life depends upon the extent to which the Christian trusts the Lord with every detail of his life, and upon his maturity in Christ. One who is only beginning to understand the ministry of the Holy Spirit should not be discouraged if he is not as fruitful as more mature Christians who have known and experienced this truth for a longer period.

*Why is it that most Christians are not experiencing the abundant life?*

# B. CARNAL CHRISTIANS CANNOT EXPERIENCE THE ABUNDANT AND FRUITFUL CHRISTIAN LIFE

The carnal man trusts in his own efforts to live the Christian life:

**1.** He is either uninformed about, or has forgotten, God's love, forgiveness and power (Romans 5:8-10; Hebrews 10:1-25; 1 John 1; 2:1-3; 2 Peter 1:9; Acts 1:8).

**2.** He has an up-and-down spiritual experience.

**3.** He cannot understand himself—he wants to do what is right, but cannot.

**4.** He fails to draw upon the power of the Holy Spirit to live the Christian life.

(1 Corinthians 3:1-3; Romans 7:15-24; 8:7; Galatians 5:16-18)

### THE CARNAL MAN

Some or all of the following traits may characterize the Christian who does not fully trust God:

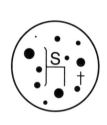

Ignorance of his
  spiritual heritage
Unbelief
Disobedience
Loss of love for God
  and for others
Poor prayer life
No desire for Bible study

Legalistic attitude
Discouragement
Impure thoughts
Jealousy
Guilt
Critical spirit
Worry
Frustration
Aimlessness

(The individual who professes to be a Christian but who continues to practice sin should realize that he may not be a Christian at all, according to 1 John 2:3; 3:6,9; Ephesians 5:5.)

*The third truth gives us the only solution to this problem...*

# C. JESUS PROMISED THE ABUNDANT AND FRUITFUL LIFE AS THE RESULT OF BEING FILLED (CONTROLLED AND EMPOWERED) BY THE HOLY SPIRIT

The Spirit-filled life is the Christ-controlled life by which Christ lives His life in and through us in the power of the Holy Spirit (John 15).

**1.** One becomes a Christian through the ministry of the Holy Spirit, according to John 3:1-8. From the moment of spiritual birth, the Christian is indwelt by the Holy Spirit at all times (John 1:12; Colossians 2:9,10; John 14:16,17). Though all Christians are indwelt by the Holy Spirit, not all Christians are filled (controlled and empowered) by the Holy Spirit.

**2.** The Holy Spirit is the source of the overflowing life (John 7:37-39).

**3.** The Holy Spirit came to glorify Christ (John 16:1-5). When one is filled with the Holy Spirit, he is a true disciple of Christ.

**4.** In His last command before His Ascension, Christ promised the power of the Holy Spirit to enable us to be witnesses for Him (Acts 1:1-9).

*How, then, can one be filled with the Holy Spirit?*

# D. WE ARE FILLED (CONTROLLED AND EMPOWERED) BY THE HOLY SPIRIT BY FAITH; THEN WE CAN EXPERIENCE THE ABUNDANT AND FRUITFUL LIFE THAT CHRIST PROMISED TO EACH CHRISTIAN

You can appropriate the filling of the Holy Spirit *right now* if you:

**1.** Sincerely desire to be controlled and empowered by the Holy Spirit (Matthew 5:6; John 7:37-39).

**2.** Confess your sins.

By faith thank God that He has forgiven all of your sins—past, present, and future—because Christ died for you (Colossians 2:13-15; 1 John 1; 2:1-3; Hebrews 10:1-17).

**3.** By faith claim the fullness of the Holy Spirit, according to:

a. HIS COMMAND—Be filled with the Spirit. "And do not get drunk with wine, for that is dissipation, but be filled with the Spirit" (Ephesians 5:18).

b. HIS PROMISE—He will always answer when we pray according to His will. "And this is the confidence which we have before Him, that, if we ask anything according to His will, He hears us. And if we know that He hears us in whatever we ask, we know that we have the requests which we have asked from Him" (1 John 5:14,15).

*Faith can be expressed through prayer...*

## How to Pray in Faith to Be Filled with the Holy Spirit

We are filled with the Holy Spirit by faith alone. However, true prayer is one way of expressing your faith. The following is a suggested prayer:

> *Dear Father, I need You. I acknowledge that I have been in control of my life; and that, as a result, I have sinned against You. I thank You that You have forgiven my sins through Christ's death on the cross for me. I now invite Christ to again take control of the throne of my life. Fill me with the Holy Spirit as You commanded me to be filled, and as You promised in your Word that You would do if I asked in faith. I pray this in the name of Jesus. As an expression of my faith, I now thank You for taking control of my life and for filling me with the Holy Spirit.*

Does this prayer express the desire of your heart? If so, bow in prayer and trust God to fill you with the Holy Spirit right now.

## How to Know that You are Filled (Controlled And Empowered) by the Holy Spirit

Did you ask God to fill you with the Holy Spirit? Do you know that you are now filled with the Holy Spirit? On what authority?

(On the trustworthiness of God Himself and His Word: Hebrews 11:6; Romans 14:22,23.)

Do not depend upon feelings. The promise of God's Word, not our feelings, is our authority. The Christian lives by faith (trust) in the trustworthiness of God Himself and His Word. This train diagram illustrates the relationship between fact (God and His Word), faith (our trust in God and His Word), and feeling (the result of our faith and obedience) (John 14:21).

The train will run with or without the caboose. However, it would be futile to attempt to pull the train by the caboose. In the same way, we, as Christians, do not depend upon feelings or emotions, but we place our faith (trust) in the trustworthiness of God and the promises of His Word.

## How to Walk in the Spirit

Faith (trust in God and His promises) is the only means by which a Christian can live the Spirit-controlled life. As you continue to trust Christ moment by moment:

1. Your life will demonstrate more and more of the fruit of the Spirit (Galatians 5:22,23); and will be more and more conformed to the image of Christ (Romans 12:2; 2 Corinthians 3:18).

2. Your prayer life and study of God's Word will become more meaningful.

3. You will experience His power in witnessing (Acts 1:8).

4. You will be prepared for spiritual conflict against the world (1 John 2:15-17); against the flesh (Galatians 5:16,17); and against Satan (1 Peter 5:7-9; Ephesians 6:10-13).

5. You will experience His power to resist temptation and sin (1 Corinthians 10:13; Philippians 4:13; Ephesians 1:19-23; 6:10; 2 Timothy 1:7; Romans 6;1-16).

## Spiritual Breathing

By faith you can continue to experience God's love and for-giveness.

If you become aware of an area of your life (an attitude or an action) that is displeasing to the Lord, even though you are walking with Him and sincerely desiring to serve Him, simply thank God that He has forgiven your sins—past, present and future—on the basis of Christ's death on the cross. Claim His love and forgiveness by faith and continue to have fellowship with Him.

If you retake the throne of your life through sin—a definite act of disobedience—breathe spiritually.

Spiritual Breathing (exhaling the impure and inhaling the pure) is an exercise in faith that enables you to continue to experience God's love and forgiveness.

1. Exhale—confess your sin—agree with God concerning your sin and thank Him for His forgiveness of it, according to 1 John 1:9 and Hebrews 10:1-25. Confession involves repen-tance—a change in attitude and action.

2. Inhale—surrender the control of your life to Christ, and appropriate (receive) the fullness of the Holy Spirit by faith. Trust that He now controls and empowers you, according to the command of Ephesians 5:18, and the promise of 1 John 5:14,15.

# Renew Your Commitment.

Y ou've just finished an inspiring study from **The HomeBuilders Couples Series™**. No doubt you've learned a lot of things about your mate that will help the two of you grow closer together for years to come. You've also learned a lot about God's Word, and how much it means to study the Bible with other couples. But don't let it stop here—lay the next block in the foundation of your marriage by beginning another **HomeBuilders** couples study. It will help you keep your marriage as strong, as dynamic, as solid as the day you said "I do."

## Your Mate Is a Gift from God.

Growing together as one begins by accepting your husband or wife as God's perfect provision for your needs —and trusting that He knows what your needs are even better than you do. Receive your mate with open arms, and you'll begin to draw closer together—in incredible, heartfelt new ways.

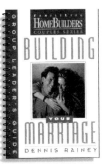

*Building Your Marriage*
*By Dennis Rainey*
*Study Guide S411172*
*Leader's Guide AB026*

## Turn Conflict into Love and Understanding.

Every marriage has its share of conflict. But you can turn conflict into something positive. Once you get into the habit of being a blessing even when you've been insulted, you'll discover for yourself that the result—a stronger, more exciting marriage—is well worth the effort.

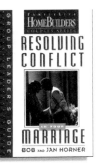

*Resolving Conflict in Your Marriage*
*By Bob & Jan Horner*
*Study Guide S411202*
*Leader's Guide AB031*

## Celebrate and Enjoy Your Differences.

Once you understand that your differences are gifts from God, you'll see how they can help you enjoy each other more and make your relationship fun, healthy and fascinating. You are the unique person who is equipped to complete and fulfill your mate!

*Building Teamwork*
*in Your Marriage*
*By Robert Lewis*
*Study Guide S411181*
*Leader's Guide AB028*

## Marriage Is God's Workshop for Self-Esteem.

When you both know you are accepted, appreciated and free to risk failure, you'll experience new levels of love and fulfillment—personally and as a couple. It starts by putting past hurts behind you and bringing positive words to your mate that will strengthen, heal and encourage. This study will show you how.

*Building Your Mate's*
*Self-Esteem*
*By Dennis & Barbara Rainey*
*Study Guide S411199*
*Leader's Guide AB030*

# "A Weekend to Remember"

Every couple has a unique set of needs. The FamilyLife Marriage Conference meets couples' needs by equipping them with proven solutions that address practically every component of "How to Build a Better Marriage." The conference gives you the opportunity to slow down and focus on your spouse and your relationship. You will spend an insightful weekend together, doing fun couples' projects and hearing from dynamic speakers on real-life solutions for building and enhancing oneness in your marriage.

**You'll learn:**

◆ *Five secrets of successful marriage*
◆ *How to implement oneness in your marriage*
◆ *How to maintain a vital sexual relationship*
◆ *How to handle conflict*
◆ *How to express forgiveness to one another*

**Our insightful speaker teams also conduct sessions for:**

◆ *Soon-to-be-marrieds*
◆ *Men-only*
◆ *Women-only*

## The FamilyLife Marriage Conference
To register or receive a free brochure and schedule, call
**FamilyLife at 1-800-333-1433.**

## FAMILYLIFE
*A ministry of Campus Crusade for Christ International*

# Take a Weekend...to Raise Your Children for a Lifetime

Good parents aren't just born that way; they begin with a strong, biblical foundation and then work at improving their parenting skills. That's where we come in.

In one weekend the FamilyLife Parenting Conference will equip you with the principles and tools you need to be more effective parents for a lifetime. Whether you're just getting started or in the turbulent years of adolescence, we'll show you the biblical blueprints for raising your children. You'll hear from dynamic speakers and do fun parenting skills projects designed to help you apply what you've learned. You'll receive proven, effective principles from parents just like you who have dedicated their lives to helping families.

**You'll learn how to:**

◆ *Build a strong relationship with your child*

◆ *Help your child develop emotional, spiritual and sexual identity*

◆ *Develop moral character in your child*

◆ *Give your child a sense of mission*

◆ *Pass on your values to your child*

## The FamilyLife Parenting Conference

To register or receive a free brochure and schedule, call **FamilyLife at 1-800-333-1433.**

## FAMILYLIFE

*A ministry of Campus Crusade for Christ International*

# FamilyLife Resources

## Building Your Mate's Self-Esteem

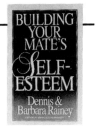

The key to a joy-filled marriage is a strong sense of self-worth in both partners. This practical, best-selling book helps you tap into God's formula for building up your mate. How to overcome problems from the past, how to help your mate conquer self-doubt, how to boost communication, and much more. Creative "Esteem-Builder Projects" will bring immediate results, making your marriage all it can be. The #1 best-seller at FamilyLife Marriage Conferences across America. **Paperback, $8.95**

## Pulling Weeds, Planting Seeds

Thirty-eight insightful, thought-provoking chapters, laced with humor, show how you can apply the wisdom of God's Word to your life and home. Includes chapters on making your time with your family count, dealing with tough situations at home and at work, living a life of no regrets, and MUCH MORE. These bite-sized, fun-to-read chapters make this great book hard to put down. **Hardcover, $12.95**

## Staying Close

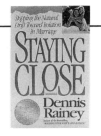

Overcome the isolation that creeps into so many marriages, and watch your marriage blossom! This best-selling book, winner of the 1990 Gold Medallion Award for best book on marriage and family, is packed with practical ideas and HomeBuilders projects to help you experience the oneness God designed for your marriage. How to manage stress. How to handle conflict. How to be a great lover. And much more! Based on 15 years of research and favorite content from the FamilyLife Marriage Conference. **Paperback, $10.95**

## The Questions Book

Discover the miracle of truly understanding each other. This book will lead you into deeper intimacy and joy by giving you 31 sets of fun, thought-provoking questions you can explore and answer together. Space is provided for you to write your answers. Share your innermost feelings, thoughts, goals, and dreams. This book could lead to the best times you'll ever spend together. **Hardcover, $9.95**

*For more information on these and other FamilyLife Resources contact your local Christian retailer or call FamilyLife at 1-800-333-1433.*

# HomeBuilders Evaluation

Your First Name _____ Last Name _____

Spouse's First Name _____ Wedding Date _____ Your Age _____

Home Phone _____ Work Phone _____

Address _____

City _____ State _____ ZIP Code _____

Full Church Name _____

Church City _____ State _____ May we quote you?

❑ Yes   ❑ No

How would you rate this HomeBuilders Couples study?

|  | Poor |   |   |   |   |   |   |   | Excellent |   |
|---|---|---|---|---|---|---|---|---|---|---|
| Overall experience | 1 | 2 | 3 | 4 | 5 | 6 | 7 | 8 | 9 | 10 |
| Study Guide | 1 | 2 | 3 | 4 | 5 | 6 | 7 | 8 | 9 | 10 |
| Leader's Guide | 1 | 2 | 3 | 4 | 5 | 6 | 7 | 8 | 9 | 10 |

How many HomeBuilders Couples Series have you now participated in ? [      ]

Describe the effect this HomeBuilders study has had on you, your family and your group:

How would you change or improve this HomeBuilders study?

Was this group formed from your: ❑ Church Community ❑ Neighborhood
❑ FamilyLife Marriage Conference ❑ FamilyLife Parenting Conference
❑ Work place   Other: _____
How many people were in this HomeBuilders group? _____
Where did you meet?   ❑ Home (s)          ❑ Church building
How often did your group meet?   ❑ Once/week      ❑ Every other week
                                 ❑ Every month     ❑ Other: _____
What day of the week would your group normally meet?
❑ Sunday Morning     ❑ Monday      ❑ Wednesday     ❑ Friday
❑ Sunday Evening     ❑ Tuesday     ❑ Thursday      ❑ Saturday
Have HomeBuilders materials been used in your church? ❑ Yes ❑ No
Have you attended a FamilyLife Conference? ❑ Yes ❑ No

Pastor's First Name _____ Last Name _____

FamilyLife has many other resources for you and your family.  Please check if you would like to receive additional information on the following resources:
❑  Other HomeBuilders Couples Series studies    ❑  "FamilyLife Today"
❑  FamilyLife Marriage Conference                   radio program
❑  FamilyLife Parenting Conference              ❑  Books, videos and tapes

# BUSINESS REPLY MAIL

FIRST-CLASS MAIL    PERMIT NO.4092    LITTLE ROCK, AR

POSTAGE WILL BE PAID BY ADDRESSEE

FAMILY LIFE
P O BOX 23840
LITTLE ROCK AR 72221-9940